Hi!

Deborah Bragg has been a journalist and flying instructor but for the last 20 years she has worked as a dog psychologist. She is the Director of the Canine Behaviour Centre and author of two other non-fiction books as well as the Dog Psychology Home Study Course. *The Forever Puppy* is based on Beau's Blog which ran on her website www.caninebehaviour.co.uk for the first year of his life with her, attracting thousands of hits.

also by Deborah Bragg:

How to Pick the Perfect Puppy ... for You

An Old Bag And An Ass

Greater Than All Things

The

Forever Puppy

an irrepressible Beau

tells his own story

Deborah Bragg

for

Titus, Rosco and Beau

I see my boy eagerly racing across the golden sand in his haste to get to the sea. He loves to surf: the wilder the wave the more he loves it. He watches as the swell approaches and then, with perfect timing, launches himself into it at the exact moment it breaks open. Again and again, he disappears into the white foam, his head emerging triumphantly a moment later.

But wait: Titus has suddenly spotted something potentially more exciting than the sea. I yell "No!" but it is too late. He is already streaking towards the unsuspecting couple on the horizon. I watch them stiffen at the sight of a black torpedo flying across the sand but then, even from a distance I can see their bodies relax and they stroke him as he dances round them, tail waving gaily. Introductions over, he races back to me.

We walk back through the dunes, secret hideout of rabbits and naked gay men. Titus pounces on both with equal glee but only the latter leap up, the air turning blue as they try to protect their private parts from a wet and sandy intruder.

7

Titus is oblivious to their distress. Tongue lolling, he grins amiably, totally convinced that they are pleased to see him and that their day would have been infinitely poorer without the experience of meeting him.

And then I wake up.

Introduction

I have owned and worked with many different breeds but Titus was my first experience of the flatcoated retriever and thanks to him, I became addicted to this extrovert, loveable, crazy, at times exasperating breed. There is something magnetic about the flatcoat that draws past and present owners together in a way that no other breed does. Oh! a flatcoat! people exclaim, please can I say hello? And then they tell you about those that they have known and loved. In true flatcoat fashion, my boys are always thrilled to be the centre of attention, tails waving ecstatically. If there is a friendlier, more outgoing breed than the flatcoated retriever I don't know of it. But they come with a warning: if you are not mad before you get one, you soon will be!

When Titus died and it came to finding flatcoat puppy number three, I would have liked to have gone back to his breeder Hilly but the litter was a one-off. So I returned to the breeder of my second flatcoat, Rosco. Sheena ticked all the boxes for me: I liked her as a person; she was extremely knowledgeable of the breed thanks to 30+ years' experience; she only had a litter when she wanted a puppy herself rather than to make money; she did not own many dogs, and her reputation as a breeder was such that she had orders for her puppies before they were even conceived. Our hopes rested on Rosco's half sister Ceili. Sadly it was not to be so Sheena decided to end her breeding line, leaving me to start from scratch finding a flatcoat puppy.

As a dog psychologist I have been doling out excellent advice on how to buy a perfect puppy for 20 years (and even written a booklet on the subject) because experience has shown me that so many later problems could have been avoided if the owners had only been a little more thorough and discriminating in their choice. For example, when buying a puppy it is essential to talk to the breeder at length on the phone before you go near the litter and if you don't like the sound of him/her to stay clear. Be prepared to shop around. You wouldn't buy the first car or house you look at so why buy the first puppy? Ideally, meet the bitch in advance and then with her puppies and preferably have first pick of the litter – not the one that nobody else wanted.

Unfortunately, when it came to buying my puppy I ignored all my own advice and let my heart rule my head.

I spoke to the hilariously named Litter Secretary of the Flat-coat Retriever Society for details of any puppies and she told me of one conveniently located in the next county. But after speaking to the breeder on the telephone I felt that this was not the litter for me. And then, the Secretary told me of a litter in Blackpool where the great great grandfather was Samson, father of my beloved Titus. All the litter had been sold except one. It was fate! I was convinced that this was meant to be. I was excited but not so carried away that I didn't seek the opinions of Sheena as well as another top flatcoat judge who knew Helen, the breeder, and had actually seen the litter. Looking back, I realise that while neither said anything derogatory about her, they didn't actually enthuse either. But we only ever hear what we want to hear! If I had followed my own advice I would have gone to see the puppy but time was running out. Easter was approaching and Helen planned on taking all her dogs and puppies to a flyball jamboree. I emphatically did not want "my" unvaccinated, almost eight week old puppy at such an event so we arranged to meet half way at a friend of hers, another flatcoat breeder. Richard, the husband of a friend of mine, nobly volunteered to come with me as puppy holder.

Three hours late, Helen finally arrived at the meeting place and my heart sank. I could not warm to her: so much for my policy of only buying from a breeder you like. I was even less impressed with the uncontrollable pack of flatcoats and wolfhound puppy that bounded out of the back of her pick-up. And my normally friendly Rosco shrank back when they greeted him. I knew that if there had been time to drive to Blackpool, I would have left empty handed.

What was I to do? I looked at Richard, bravely smiling as smelly flatcoats jumped all over him and wondered whether I had the nerve to tell him the eight hour round trip was all for nothing. And send the adorable but unnaturally calm puppy – sedated or shell shocked? – back to Blackpool? To hell with it, how could I reject him simply on the basis of my and Rosco's instinctive reactions? So, with huge misgivings I wrote the cheque, settled him on Richard's knee and we headed for home.

11

The next day an almost eight week old puppy started writing his blog…

Hi I'm Beau

My name is Ravencrag Fly Me To The Moon but since you'd feel a bit of a prat shouting such a mouthful across the countryside, I'm Beau because I am such a beautiful boy. (Can fellas be "beautiful" or is it only girls?) My mum Delilah told me weeks ago that one day I would have to leave home for a new place and she gave me lots of advice that, frankly, I didn't bother to listen to. If I had, I might not have found yesterday such a shock. I travelled with my old boss Helen and her husband Chris in the front of the car while in the back were my mum, my granny Bounty and grandpa Rocket plus an Irish wolfhound puppy called Ava. It was a very long drive and I got a bit fed up so I spent the time either in the footwell or hanging over Helen's shoulder. Eventually we got to someone's house where there were even more flatcoats and loads of noise. And there I met my new boss, Deborah – known as Boss from now on. I had a quick piddle and then I got into another car sitting on the lap of a very nice man called Richard. In the back was my new housemate, Rosco. Finally, after nearly four hours we made it to my new home which seems pretty nice. Rosco is not very friendly at the moment. I would so love to play with him but he tends to grumble at me if I get too close. In the evening I curled up on the sofa with Boss. She talked very softly about all sorts of things to come: walks on the beach here and in the mountains of Spain, learning to be a gundog and going to shoots. I didn't understand a word but I liked hearing her murmur to me and soon fell asleep. She took me out into the garden at about

11pm and then tucked me into my new bed. I suppose I could have cried for my mum but I was too tired to bother; I just slept solidly until she reappeared about 6am. She played with me and then left me all alone while she and Rosco went for a walk. Then they came home and later we had a few visitors which I loved because they made a big fuss of me. I think Rosco was a bit miffed that I was getting all the attention! I love exploring this great big garden although I have learned that I am not supposed to prune the roses and I am absolutely not allowed to yank Rosco's tail, however tempting it seems. So much to discover and learn and I haven't even been here 24 hours yet! I'm tired out now so I'll tell you more in a day or two...

My daily routine

I've only been in my new home a few days but already I feel very settled and happy with a definite routine. I wake Boss up just before 6am but she forgives me because then I do an enormous piddle on the grass – rather than inside. (At the moment my bed is inside a pen in the kitchen. Boss says it's until she can be sure Rosco won't hurt me but eventually I shall sleep next to him under the table in the dining room). Then it's time for breakfast, then out again for a poo and another piddle. Then I play around for a while before Boss disappears up above and comes down dressed. We play in the garden for a little until I am tired and then Boss puts me in my bed and takes Rosco for a walk. Being left doesn't bother me at all; I just go to sleep. The rest of the day is made up of food, sleep and play. Rosco still isn't very friendly but Boss tells me to be patient, that it's early days but she also points out that he would like me a little better if I didn't bite him. But it is soooooooooo much fun! Sometimes he lets me get quite close before growling and rushing off. Just let him wait until I am big enough to catch him! I have had more visitors. The most recent were some children who were very gentle with me. Well, they were until I got a bit over-excited and started biting and pulling their hair.

Gardening

Boss spent a lot of the weekend gardening. I really enjoyed helping her: weeding and then, when the barrow was full, helping to empty it. (Apparently it was meant to end up on the rubbish heap – not scattered all over the lawn). When I got bored with that, I went on safari. Some of the garden is lawn and flower bed but there is a lot that is like a jungle. Then I heard Boss calling "Beau? Where are you?" and I bounced out "Here I am!" She laughed and scooped me up and told me I'm a good boy for coming when called. I've discovered that Boss is pretty laid back which is just as well as this morning I jumped in the laundry basket just as she was going to peg out the washing. Her white sheets now have little muddy paw prints all over them but she didn't seem too bothered. But I am learning that there are some things I am absolutely *not* to do: chew the books, pull the fringe of the Afghan rug, sharpen my teeth on the furniture or swing off the pendulum of the cuckoo clock. She never actually says "No!" – instead, she just goes "uh-uh" and finds me something else to play with. And I soon forget because, as she says, I have the attention span of a gnat.

Visit to the vet

Today I went to the vet for my first vaccination. Boss put a bit of my mum's old bed in the footwell but I didn't want to sit down there. I climbed on to the passenger seat and cried. This wasn't at all like the long drive a week ago when I had nice Richard to cuddle and comfort me. The more I cried, the hotter and thirstier I got but Boss had taken some water which was a relief. When we got there, vet Jenny offered me a treat but I didn't want one at first because it was all so confusing – was I changing homes *again*? - and I just clung on tight to Boss. But then I realised that Jenny was really very nice and gentle and since she'd left the pot of treats on the table I stuck my head in and attempted to scoff the lot before she hurriedly removed it. On the way home I fell fast asleep – on the seat, not the footwell.

My new best friend

Yesterday Bella, a golden retriever, and her boss Barbara came to play. Bella is like a huge cuddly blonde bear; she let me climb all over her and chew her plumy tail. I was really sad when it was time for them to go and wondered whether we could swap her for grumpy old Rosco but no such luck. But Boss has promised we shall see her again soon.

"Sit!"

I am a little more than eight weeks old but already I have learned to sit when I am told. To be honest, if this is what training is all about, then it's a doddle! Boss moved her hand back over my head and rather than get a crick in my neck I sat down just as she said "Sit." Then I got a treat. You don't have to be Mastermind to work this one out. Quick as a flash now, as soon as she says "Sit", I sit. Yesterday just the two of us went on a little outing as Boss says I have to start getting used to lots of different experiences, including the car. She put me in the footwell and I promptly tried to climb on the seat. But she was very firm and said I had to stay down below. I whinged for a bit and then we stopped at a garden centre where she carried me into the shop. One cashier made a big fuss of me but the other one was a bit worried because they sell food and I shouldn't have been in there, even in Boss's arms. On the way home I settled down, didn't cry and didn't try to climb on the seat. Boss says that ideally I should be travelling in the back but until she can trust Rosco I will have to stay in the front. But she says anyway it's useful to have a dog that will sit in the footwell if the back is full. When visitors called round at the weekend they said "Goodness, hasn't he grown!" (Silly comment: what do they expect me to do? Shrink?) I know I must have grown because when I arrived I couldn't see into Rosco's food bowl (he has his on a stand) and now I nearly can!

A day in the life

I have been here two weeks now and I am learning that life as a nine and a half week old puppy is hugely exciting. There is something new to discover and learn every day. It's not always nice – like when there was a loud bang in the garden which gave me a terrible fright

17

and sent me running for the back door. But then I noticed that Boss just carried on weeding and Rosco didn't even raise his head (he was sunbathing at the time) so I stopped and thought maybe there wasn't anything to worry about after all. The list of things I am *not* to do grows daily: pounce on Rosco when he is minding his own business in his bed, pick the flowers (those geraniums were just begging to be beheaded), and try and catch the bees that buzz on the grass. But mostly Boss seems pretty pleased with me. She says it was serendipity that she found me; that we were meant to be together. Like my eight brothers I had been chosen but then my would-be owner changed her mind, apparently because I had been chipped. Boss is not convinced that's the truth but she says, whatever, it was lucky for us both. Every morning after breakfast she plays with me and Rosco, then washes up and hoovers (I was scared of this at first but now I try to stalk it) before she goes out for a two or three hour walk with Rosco and I catch up on sleep. Then it's more play before lunchtime. In the afternoon sometimes people call round or we go for a little drive but Boss always spends some time with me on my own. This is *me* time. I'm not very interested in supper but Boss says I must have three meals a day so she puts my kibble in a flying saucer toy. This is a great way to eat as I have to work very hard, spinning it and turning it upside down to get the food out. When I am completely exhausted with racing round the room there is nothing I like more than to lie at the base of Boss's armchair and go to sleep with my head on her foot. That means I know if she gets up to go somewhere because I still sleep the sleep of the dead – unlike Rosco who always has an ear or eye open. Finally, when it's dark the two of us go outside for a last piddle and then I settle down in my bed and dream of another thrilling day to come.

Playmate at last?

I think – paws crossed – that Rosco is beginning to like me a little. Outside, he has started to play with me; sometimes he dangles a toy just above my head tempting me to jump for it which usually means I end up head over heels. Although he is really ancient – I can't imagine being as old as seven – he is very playful and is always getting something out of our toy box for Boss to play with him. We sniff noses and he lets me jump at his face now but his ears must be a bit tender because he goes ballistic if I grab one. If I promise not to bite, he lets me sit quite close to him but only in the garden – never indoors. In the evening when I have my wild hour tearing around I check that Boss has her nose in a book and then I try stalking Rosco in his bed. But from the armchair comes "Beau!" in that warning tone of voice I am learning means "Don't even think about it!" Does she have eyes in the back of her head? So I leave off and wait for another opportunity (when she's distracted on the phone is usually a good time) and collapse in a heap on Boss's feet.

Perfect – but determined

I am 10 weeks old today and every day I grow bigger and bolder. I can now get on the armchair by myself, see out of the window if I hang on tight to the windowsill (it's not really my fault if I knock the ornaments off – it's a dumb place to put them) and drink the water in Rosco's bowl on the stand. I can also sit when I'm told, come when I'm called (if I'm not too busy) and cock a leg when I piddle. Talking of which, I always wait until Boss finally bestirs herself around 8am with no accidents during the night; in fact I haven't had a pee in the house since the first week and I've never ever done a poo indoors. I reckon I'm pretty perfect! Boss, on the other hand, says I'm absolutely enchanting when I am asleep and a complete pain in the neck in the evening because I am totally OTT. But the only thing that really worries her is my habit of eating dead grass; she says it could make me seriously ill because there is sweet clover in it. She tries everything to stop me: ignoring me, distraction, grabbing me, sneaking up on me, smacking a newspaper just behind me or clapping her hands loudly. Any or all of this stops me for a moment and then, when she isn't looking, I sneak back for another mouthful. Determined is my middle name; actually Boss says something that is considerably less complimentary...

Best buddies

Rosco definitely likes me now - we spent the Bank Holiday weekend playing for hours on end. Sometimes he lies down and lets me jump on him (occasionally he forgets I'm there and nearly rolls on top of me!), otherwise we play bite each other. Although he's so much bigger than me, he's lots of fun – although I do get a bit scared when he starts the lapping the garden at 500mph. And I get quite dizzy when he spins round and round in front of me. I'm so grown up now that the pen has gone back into the shed and Boss leaves me the run of the ground floor when she goes out. But at night I still have to stay in the kitchen just in case I get carried away and try to bite Rosco where Boss says no chap wants to be bitten.

Pluses and minuses

Pride comes before a piddle ... this will teach me to boast that I was pretty perfect. Yesterday evening I had not one, not two, but three mishaps on the dining room carpet. Boss was disappointed rather than cross and said she couldn't understand how I could last from 10pm until 7am or 8am – and then have an accident after just 20 minutes. I think it was a case of getting over excited playing with Rosco and just forgetting where I was. And it *was* raining outside! On the plus side not only can I sit with no reward (a bit mean of Boss but I am ever hopeful) I can also shake hands. She says "shake hands" and I put my big fat paw in hers.

Such a social life!

Boss is determined to get me used to the car so we have been going on lots of little outings. We went to a plant centre where a woman, seeing Boss was struggling to hold me under one arm and pick up tomato plants with the other, offered to hold me. (I still can't go down on the ground where other, possibly unvaccinated, dogs have been). She took me all around and introduced me to everyone. Yesterday we went to see Boss's friend Chris where I explored her garden and very nearly managed to catch one of her tame pheasants before Boss grabbed me by the tail. I was fascinated by the pond and paddled my front paws in the water but decided I wasn't ready for a swim just yet. While they had coffee I found myself a fir cone which I chewed under the kitchen table before falling fast asleep. A social life is very exhausting you know... In the afternoon there was a thunderstorm which was really scary. There was a loud crack and then a bang but Rosco didn't seem bothered and Boss just went on reading the paper. It did occur to me that they are both deaf. Just as I was beginning to think perhaps it was OK there was another crash bang so I tucked myself between Boss's legs for safety – not that she paid any attention to me, she just went on reading. This morning I went to church. Boss has a thing about Suffolk churches so I suspect I shall be visiting a lot more but today we met up with lots of other women who all oohed and aahed over me – at first. They were less impressed when I forgot myself in the excitement and had a piddle in the aisle. And then there was a moment of panic when I got my head stuck between the altar rails. I yelled and screamed until Boss came and eased me out. I suppose this is what they mean about lots to learn. Like not putting your head where a head isn't meant to go.

Chill!

On a hot day when you've finished digging and replanting and using your best mate as a trampoline, there's only one thing left to do – and that's to chillax in the armchair...

22

Woof

Today I barked for the very first time! I was so surprised I looked round to see where it had come from – before realising it was me! I had been trying to pounce on the hoover when this funny noise came out of my mouth. It was like a cross between a yelp and a grumble; certainly nothing like Rosco's "Beware" bark which is so loud and deep that even though I know it's not directed at me it always makes me jump and rush indoors. I suppose one day I too will have a big deep bark to frighten people away.

Big boy

I am now 12 weeks old and at 10 kilos I am a big, big boy. I'm not fat but "chunky" according to vet Jenny. So much so that she asked Boss if I was actually a Newfoundland puppy rather than a flatcoat. What a cheek! But I decided to forgive her because she said I had "a really beautiful head." Boss says it will be a relief when I can finally go down on the ground in a week's time and she no longer has to lug me around.

Sorry, sorry, sorry

The recent heat has really knocked me out. I spend most of the day asleep in the cool indoors which means that when it comes to the evening, I am full of beans. Yesterday Boss was sitting on the grass making a fuss of Rosco and I thought it would be fun to sneak up on her and grab a chunk of hair. She let out a great yell – clearly a humour failure on her part. I tried to make up for it later by getting a big pot out of the greenhouse, carrying it ever so carefully across the lawn, in the back door, down the big step into the kitchen and into the dining room without spilling a drop. Unfortunately in the excitement of presenting Boss with my gift, I tripped and upended the compost and fuschia all over the pale green carpet. The world's most popular puppy, not....Then, I amused myself dragging Rosco's bed outside and trying to provoke him into playing with me. I could hear Boss warning me to leave him alone but I ignored her. Suddenly Rosco turned on me and I fled outside with a yelp. He didn't actually hurt me at all but he gave me a fright as he doesn't usually tell me off so sternly. I crept back, tail wagging and tried to say sorry but he just walked off. Boss picked me up for a cuddle and sighed, "One day Beau you'll learn that if you play with fire, you get burnt."

Out – at last!

Today was the day when I was finally allowed to make my public debut! Boss took Rosco for his normal walk and then came home and collected me and took us to the seaside. It was *such* fun. I found some fish scales to roll in and then a great big fish head which I tried to eat but, quick as a flash, Boss confiscated it. I liked watching the waves crashing on the stones and tried to drink some of the water but it tasted funny. After playing for a while we went to the garden centre where last time the woman carried me. But this time I used my legs. (Rosco stayed in the car with the tailgate open). This was my first time on the lead so I pulled and jumped up and down for a bit which made people giggle but then I realised it was less exhausting just to walk alongside Boss. Lots of people stopped and said hello to me and one woman said, "Isn't he good that he doesn't jump up?" Little did she know that I would have done normally but I was just sooooo tired it was easier to sit down and be fussed over. On the way home I forgot I don't like the car and went fast asleep.

The devil finds work for idle paws

Normally Boss takes Rosco out for a walk quite early which fits in well with my nap time. But this morning it was raining and hoping it would stop, she decided instead to defrost the freezer and then talk at length on the phone with a friend who is coming to visit next weekend. (Whoopppeee – hopefully more members of my ever-growing fan club). So by the time she finally left I was wide awake and very, very bored. I climbed on a chair and then on to the dining room table. I thought I'd pretend I was Boss, reading the newspaper with her glasses... I have absolutely no idea how the paper ended up shredded and the glasses a bit bent. Boss was less than ecstatic when she returned. She didn't actually tell me off and she can't have been that cross – can she? – as she then took me across the Common. I walked a little bit on the lead and then she let me play in the long grass and we practised me coming when she called.

A poorly me – a poor Boss

Boss loathes Bank Holiday weekends because there are lots of people everywhere. She normally refuses to leave the house but this one was going to be an exception: out to a BBQ lunch and Rosco and I were on the guest list! But it didn't happen because on Saturday afternoon I started to be very sick. On Sunday Boss came down at

5am and found me lying in vomit. She cleaned me up and then I rushed outside with horrible diarrhoea. I felt absolutely awful so Boss rang the emergency vet and she saw me at 6am. She gave me two injections and discussed admitting me to the hospital. I didn't like the sound of that at all so I gave her my paw to hold, as Boss taught me, and she was so amused she agreed to let me go home on the understanding that if I was sick again I would have to go back and stay in. In the afternoon Richard came to see me which cheered me up lots but then I crawled back into my bed. That evening I felt a little better but on Monday I was sick again and I still had a runny tummy. I felt utterly listless and spent the day lying in bed feeling sorry for myself. Meanwhile Boss worked in the garden, checking on me regularly and Rosco sat around looking fed up. Boss rang the vet again and she suggested a drink of lemon juice, salt and bicarbonate of soda, and some chicken stock. By the evening I felt much better and lapped up the stock without being sick. Even the lemon drink wasn't too bad. This morning I feel much, much better but I'm still only allowed a little to eat to let my tummy heal. Boss is boiling chicken and rice for me at this very moment. I feel a bit weak and wobbly but that's probably because I've eaten hardly anything in the last three days. I'm no longer "chunky" but quite skinny! Boss says, "In future, if you're going to be ill, please can you do it in normal surgery hours." The bill was nearly £200 so she's feeling pretty poor at the moment – while I feel much better!

Back in the swing

I am now 100% again and I think Boss is wondering whether life was more peaceful when I was at death's door! I seem to hear the word "off" all the time: *off* the table, *off* the work surface, *off* the grill (only just missed grabbing a lovely hot sausage), *off* people (I am not supposed to jump up but how else can I get a look in?), *off* the flower bed. Yesterday was Boss's birthday so the house was a social whirl and I made the most of the celebrations: leaving shoes and cushions outside in the rain, pulling wrapping paper off the table, trying to get in the fridge for a piece of birthday cake, and the dishwasher for a spit and polish. Despite all the yummy food around Rosco and I didn't get a single scrap. Rosco says he hasn't been offered a titbit in *seven* years which is a bit miserable. It's policies like this that turn law abiding dogs into desperate burglars. But at least we are still eating chicken and rice to make my tummy well.

Because I'm worth it...

Yesterday the rotten sickness and diarrhoea returned. I spent most of the day curled up in the armchair feeling miserable and only going outside to be ill, one end or the other. So in the afternoon Boss took me back to the vet and this time we saw Jenny. She said I was a borderline case for admission so I wrapped both my paws round Boss's neck, begging her to say no. "Aaaah," went Jenny, "he's trying to tell us something." (I'm getting really good at eliciting the sympathy vote). They agreed on a compromise: blood tests which would show whether I needed to be admitted or not. I was a bit worried as Jenny led me away: had I misunderstood and they were going to keep me in after all? You can imagine my relief when Jenny took me back to the waiting room and I saw Boss sitting there! While we were waiting for the results, a black Labrador came in, also called Beau. He lunged and leaped around and Boss said she hoped that I'm not going to be that unruly when I get to six months old. The results showed that I was losing a little protein and the white blood cells were outside the normal range but I didn't have to be admitted. Phew! As Boss paid the bill – over £100 – she said, "You're turning out to be the most expensive puppy in the world. But you're worth it – I suppose." This morning I don't feel 100% but I do feel much better so I have to hope that the antibiotics finally clear up the infection and I can get back to beating up Rosco as usual.

The Boss

Some of you have been emailing asking if I am still ill because I have not been keeping my blog up to date. The truth of the matter is I am up and down. Friends from the north came for the weekend and I was on top form. Then on Monday I felt horrible again and spent the day curled up, refusing to eat. Early evening Boss took me and Rosco up to the heath where we wandered a little way in the sunshine (I'm not big enough to go for real walks, let alone well enough) and that cheered me up a little. On Tuesday I felt much better and Rosco and I played for ages as usual and my favourite friend Richard came round to see how I was. In the afternoon Angela came with some belated birthday presents for Boss including a tin of mints that says, "The Boss – and always will be!" on it. She has proudly propped it on the kitchen windowsill to ensure that Rosco and I never forget our places in life. Talk about encouraging her delusions...

Off to school

Bearing in mind what Boss has been doing for a living for 20+ years, you might wonder why she would take me to classes rather than home school me herself. But she says I need to learn some manners around other dogs – ie not pull their tails or jump on them – and she is always ready to learn and listen to new ideas. This morning she went to the first class *without me*. I know she's getting a bit old and dotty but even so.... But apparently the first class was puppy-less so that everybody could discover what the classes would involve without distractions. Boss says she liked Lesley who runs the classes, probably because she simply confirmed a lot of what Boss has been saying about basic training to her clients for years although they do appear to be adrift on a couple of things: for example, wearing a half check collar and the use of titbits for everything. I think the latter sounds terrific, especially since Lesley recommends the use of treats like cheese and sausages not just while we are puppies but *forever*. When Boss objected Lesley asked her if she would work for nothing and Boss said, yes, if she enjoyed the work and was appreciated. Personally I prefer Lesley's way of thinking but Boss says she has no intention of going for a walk with a bum bag stuffed with edible goodies. Shame! Instead, she thinks Rosco and I should come back for a reward in the form of praise; so it's not really working for nothing is Boss's argument. Looks like they will have to agree to differ: I won't be wearing a half check collar and it doesn't look like I'll be getting much in the way of sausages.

Let sleeping puppies lie!

It's been really hot here over the weekend which knocks me for six. Rosco seems indifferent to the heat but then he hasn't got a thick fluffy coat like mine. I thought it was supposed to be puppies that want to play all day – not seven year olds. There I am lying flat out and again and again he comes and dangles a toy over my head knowing perfectly well that I won't be able to resist jumping up and grabbing it. Hasn't he heard of letting sleeping puppies lie?

Learning all the time

The last two days have been a whirlwind of exciting new experiences. Yesterday Boss and I went to a garage and while they were fitting new tyres we walked along the pavement as big lorries swooshed past – a bit too close for my liking. This was my first experience of traffic at close quarters. A man at the garage recognised that I was a flatcoat (most people ask, "What is *it*?") and said I was an exceptionally handsome fella. In the afternoon Boss decided to water the garden with the hose. Oh what fun! I spent ages jumping into the spray and trying to bite the water and ended up looking as though I'd had a bath. In the evening we went to a different training class from Lesley's – just to see. There were three grown up dogs and a very little eight month old something or other that yapped at me. Anne, the trainer, is very flexible and accommodating (she says it's entirely up to Boss what type of collar and reward she chooses to use) but the problem is there aren't any puppies! So it looks as if we will be going to Lesley's class after all. Today I had my first visit to a pub for lunch where they say they welcome "dogs and muddy boots." While Boss and her friend Gwen stuffed their faces, I lay fast asleep under the table. Gwen isn't the type to throw out many compliments but even she admitted how well behaved I was! PS I am very grown up now. At 15 ½ weeks I usually ride in the back of the car with Rosco and I no longer have to sleep by myself in the kitchen. Now my bed is next to Rosco's under the dining room table.

In the doghouse

Whoops! A fall from grace today. I got caught in the act of picking Boss's very best roses. She was so proud of the bush that she had invited Richard and Angela round for drinks to admire its many blooms. Not anymore. S'pose this is what being a puppy is all about: flavour of the week one minute, vandal in the doghouse the next.

School is FUN!

Yesterday we went to the first training class – second time for Boss but first for me. There were nine other puppies, most of which are a little older than me. I made special friends with Pippa the labradoodle who is a big flirt with us boys, Rowley an English setter who is bigger than me but very soft, and Reuben a cocker spaniel. We worked in small groups at a time and did the "look at me" exercise,

31

the "sit", the "down" (this was new to me) and "get in your bed." Afterwards Boss and Reuben's boss stood chatting for ages in the car park and agreed to meet up for a pup play and pub lunch. Brilliant idea! Then this morning Boss, Rosco and I went to the seaside. Normally, as you know, she takes Rosco on his own for a walk but because the forecast was for a really scorching day she decided to take us both before it was too hot. Rosco spent his time hunting for stones that Boss threw in the sea while I paddled, then sat and watched him swimming, Considering I was only paddling, I'm not sure how I got quite so wet....

It's a puppy's life

I haven't been keeping up my blog lately because there doesn't seem to have been much to report. Daily life goes on pretty much the same. Every morning I get left home alone while Boss takes Rosco for a walk. If it's hot I spend most of the day asleep and then race around in the evening. Some days the three of us go and sit in the sunshine on the beach or on the heath or in the forest. Every day Boss spends a short time reminding me what "sit" and "down" mean but I'm also learning other words during the course of the day, like "wait" because I'm not allowed to get out of the car until I'm told (I like the car so much now that sometimes if the door is open I go and sit in the footwell in the hope that we go somewhere); "leave" as in don't touch the nibbles and glasses of wine on the table when friends are round for drinks; "out" when I bring a lovely chunk of dirty wood indoors, and of course the everlasting "off" for people, flower beds, the table, the armchair and so on. Sometimes I walk on the lead when I have to remember that I am supposed to keep on Boss's left and not trip her up by suddenly swinging in front of her because there is a delicious smell on the other side. And however excited I am to get a move on, I am not to pull Boss's arm out of its socket. It might seem pretty dull but it's all loads of fun and generally, paws crossed, I stay out of trouble.

Exhausted!

Going to school is *exhausting*! Actually it's not the class itself that wears me out but the playing with Reuben while we are waiting to go in. He may be much smaller than me but he's just as much of a thug! I think our respective bosses are quite embarrassed as all the other puppies sit as good as gold while the two of us have a ball jumping on each other and rolling in the dirt. Today we did quite a bit of lead walking. I gave a very good impression of trotting alongside and sitting when Boss stopped – largely because I was tired, if I am honest – but Boss still wouldn't give me a treat even though Lesley said I deserved one. We also did "vet checks" where each boss had to look in their puppy's ears and mouth and inspect their paws, and the "look at me" exercise. Then we did recall where Lesley put me on a long line while Boss went to the other end of the hall and called me. On one run I did contemplate veering off to see a very pretty cockerpoo but Boss had her arms open wide to ensure I didn't. Huh! - didn't get a treat for that either. Slept all the way home in the back of the car and most of the afternoon too.

15 love – to Boss

Boss hardly ever watches television but yesterday afternoon she sat glued to it just because some people were tossing a ball about. I was soooooo bored. I brought a log in to chew but got told to take it straight out and then I got yelled at for trying to see what was on the kitchen table. Finally she agreed to take me and Rosco to the beach for fish and chips. We had only been out of the car for five minutes when the heavens opened. I'd never seen such a heavy downpour – the most I've ever seen is what comes out of the hosepipe. (I can't think why humans say it's raining cats and dogs – it was just a lot of water, that's all). Boss ran back to the car and Rosco jumped in. She called me but I didn't want to go back; after all, we'd only just got there. I was rather hoping that Boss would try to catch me so I could run away which would have been a great game. But she's smarter than that. Instead, she climbed into the back of the car with Rosco and they started eating the fish and chips. She offered me some and I was very tempted because it smelled yummy but my pride was at stake here. So I sat and watched the seagulls who were hanging around hoping for a chip or two, pretending that I couldn't hear, getting wetter and wetter. Eventually the two of them finished eating and Boss got out, calmly scooped me up in a towel – there comes a time when you are so cold and sodden that admitting defeat is the only option – and put me in the back of the car. And the greedy pigs hadn't left me even one greasy chip as consolation! Boss says she will have to invest in a long line if I am going to be so rebellious. But

I think she should realise she's pretty lucky: I don't make a fuss when I'm left alone, I don't bite (other bosses in the class are covered in scars and ripped clothes) and I haven't chewed anything (well, only the occasional newspaper that was lying on the floor). I can't be perfect all the time ... toddler tantrums are *normal*!

Playdate

Today we met up with Reuben and his boss Clare for a romp and paddle at the beach before going for lunch in the pub. Although Reuben is older and smaller than me, for some reason he always seems to be on top.

Competitive bosses

Third week at class and it seems that all the bosses are getting very competitive – except mine and Reuben's who seem very relaxed. All the others have been madly practising and are keen to show off. Boss says I am only 18 weeks old, that there's no hurry and that she's happy for me to enjoy just being a puppy. Suits me... Today all the bosses had to groom their puppies. I was really helpful and lay on my back for Boss to tickle my tummy which apparently wasn't quite what Lesley had in mind. Then we did a bit of heelwork but to be honest I was much more interested in sniffing the floor which had all sorts of good smells (there is a class before ours and they had obviously enjoyed loads of tasty titbits). Finally we did the "wait" where Boss threw a treat on the floor in front of me, told me to wait and then that I could have it. By this time I was a little bit bored and tired (having to pay attention for a whole hour is jolly hard work) so I was much more interested in looking at what everybody else was doing. I know I'm usually quite greedy but when other things are happening, food loses its appeal. Oh yes – and we did the "off" – ie don't jump up. I don't jump up at Boss any more but I am guilty of throwing myself sky high (you wouldn't believe how long I am at full stretch!) at visitors which Boss says is totally unacceptable.

Wait for me!

When we are out walking (still not very far to protect my developing joints) Rosco hurtles off ahead and I struggle to keep up as he has no intention of waiting for me. So I usually just sit down and wait for Boss to catch up or Rosco to come back. This morning Boss took us for a short stroll by the river and at one point Rosco picked up the scent of a pheasant and disappeared. I tried to follow him but he went so fast that I lost him in reeds that were very tall and thick. I couldn't see where he was or where I was going and had a quick moment of panic. But I retraced my steps and got myself back on the path and then, oh help! I couldn't see Boss. I hurriedly set off – in the wrong direction – but then I heard Boss whistling. I turned round and was so relieved to see her and Rosco waiting for me. Phew! We haven't done any whistle training yet so this was my first introduction to the pip-pip-pip which I now know means "come."

Whistle work

Since I am now such a good boy at walking on the lead and stopping and sitting when Boss says "Sit!" (yes, really), she decided to introduce me to the "stop" whistle. We walk, she stops, says "Sit" and blows one blast on the whistle. Easy peasy! Within a little while, I was sitting just on the whistle rather than her saying anything. Mind you, I do have to concentrate. I don't always notice if she has stopped if there are things happening around me.

A future as a comedian?

Another playdate with my friend Reuben. Again we met at Dunwich and walked at the back of the beach where there are pools of lovely stinking water. Reuben showed me up by retrieving perfectly; to Boss's chagrin I preferred eating some manky green weed to fetching sticks. While I was rolling on the bank, I fell head first into the water which made Boss and Clare fall about laughing, so much so that they nearly fell in themselves. Then, more chortling when I tried to swim which I don't seem to have got the hang of: I paddle up and down with my front legs making an awful lot of noise and go absolutely nowhere. Boss says if I don't make the grade as a retriever perhaps I can earn my living as a comic. Then we went to the pub for lunch although I don't know why they call it lunch. We were there for *hours* – those two could talk for England. Reuben got a bit bored but I was happy to sleep under the table. In fact I was so deeply asleep when the barman brought our biscuits that I had to be prodded awake for mine.

Hitching a ride

Another pub lunch, another attempt at swimming, another exhausting day but this time with Boss's friend Barbara and Bella the golden retriever. We met them at a pub and had a lovely walk along the river but Bella had to stay on the lead because she adores lying in mud and Barbara thought she might get stuck in it. Then we dogs lay in the shade under the table while they ate. I was dying to say hello to all the others dogs there but Boss kept me firmly in place. Finally the bosses finished eating and the three of us went swimming in the river. Or, more accurately, Rosco went swimming, Bella sat down and washed her face and I tried swimming but since as usual I didn't go anywhere despite my frantic doggy paddle, I hitched a ride by grabbing Rosco's tail and he towed me in. It was a brilliant if tiring day and I slept soundly all the way home, dreaming that one day I will learn to swim like Rosco.

Back to the vet

After two terrific days, not such a nice one today as Rosco and I went to the vet. Rosco simply had his booster but Boss asked Jenny to look at three things with me. Lesley had said my nails needed cutting but Jenny disagreed so that was all right. Then she had a feel for my testicles which have still not appeared but she said she could feel two so they might drop soon. So far, so good. Then my luck ran out because Boss told Jenny she had noticed for some time now that I have a funny walk (other people have started to comment on it so she felt she couldn't ignore it any longer). Jenny watched me walk across the reception area and agreed. She said it could be OCD. Boss looked incredulous but Jenny hurriedly explained that she didn't mean obsessive compulsive disorder but something called osteochondrosis. Or possibly hip dysplasia. The only way to find out was to X ray my hips and knees so next Wednesday Boss has to take me in and leave me there for the day. I really don't like the sound of that so please wish me luck. To cheer us all up, afterwards Boss took us down to a meadow where cows had been. My first experience of cow pats – oh, yum yum! Something tell me we won't be going there again in a hurry!

Colour prejudice

Today we met up with Reuben for play and pub lunch. I was so miffed at Boss saying I was useless as a retriever last week that I decided to show her she shouldn't be so quick to judge and condemn. She threw a stick into the water for Reuben but it was *me* who retrieved it! True, I didn't take it back to Boss but you can't have everything. She and Clare were so surprised and obviously thought it was a fluke so they threw another and another. Each time *I* went and got it so perhaps I do have a future as a working gun dog. In the pub lots of people made a fuss of Reuben and didn't seem to notice me. It seems that this is because I'm black and people are naturally drawn to paler colours. It's the same when we are out with blondie Bella: they always make a beeline for her rather than me or Rosco. Boss says I just have to get used to such unfair prejudice but throwing myself at them in an attempt to get noticed is not the answer.

Hip problem

Nasty start to the day. Rosco and I went out for our piddles as usual, came back in and Boss made herself a coffee as she always does. But where were our bowls? Rosco and I bounced around trying to tell her she'd forgotten our breakfast but she just smiled at us and took her coffee upstairs. Then, to add insult to injury, she sat down and ate *her* breakfast in front of us! It seems I wasn't allowed to eat before my X rays and Boss rightly guessed that I would go mental if Rosco had his breakfast so he had to starve too. At the vet's Boss asked if she could stay with me until they were ready to sedate me and then wait in reception until I came round rather than leave me there for the day. She bought me a new toy and we played fetch until they were ready for me. I felt very dozy when I came round to find myself in a little cage with a blanket over me. But Boss soon appeared and she and Jenny looked at the X rays together. It seems that I have hip dysplasia in both hips, although the left is worse than the right, and that's why I walk in a funny way. Jenny is going to send the pictures off to an orthopaedic specialist who will decide what, if anything, needs to be done. Meanwhile I've had a little scrambled egg and pasta and now I'm going to sleep for the rest of the afternoon.

Back to school

After a half term break, it was back to school. We did two "wait" exercises: one where Boss had to drop the lead, walk away and then call me to her, and another where she told me to wait while she opened a gate and stepped through. Although I'd never done this before, I decided to behave impeccably – partly because poor old Boss was feeling a bit crushed after the news about my hips (she's sad not only about the pain and expense that lie ahead but worried that I may never be able to enjoy the things that she and Rosco love to do like hiking in the mountains) and partly because I just like being contrary. Confounding expectations is hard wired into all flat-coats! I don't know who was more amazed at my award winning performance: Boss, Lesley or her assistant Liz. Then we walked round the other puppies and were told to "leave" and after that everybody swapped dogs. I was paired with the boss of Tarn, a border terrier. What luck! She had a bum bag full of goodies – I'd have stayed with her all day given half a chance. I don't think Tarn was quite so impressed with my food-free Boss! At five months old I am now a very handsome fella despite my wonky hips. I'm not yet as tall as Rosco but getting there and I weigh in at 17 kilos. As my fluffy teddy bear look is being replaced by a smooth glossy coat, everyone says I am at last beginning to look like a real flatcoat rather than a bear cub.

Knees up!

The orthopaedic report is in. They are not too worried about my hips at this stage but apparently I have bowed femurs resulting in luxating patellas (or kneecaps, as you or I know them). So they have said that Boss is to slow down my growth by putting me on Rosco's adult food rather than puppy food, stop the calcium supplement and no long walks (which I didn't have anyway). Then they are going to X ray me again when I am a year old. In the meantime I shall continue walking in my funny way. After all, I am a flatcoat and so I like to be distinctively different!

Beau-legged

Boss's friend Gwen brought her sister Joi round to meet me. They were talking about my bowed femurs and Joi said, "He's got the right name, hasn't he?" Boss and Gwen looked a bit blank for a moment and then the penny dropped: bow-legged, beau-legged. They thought it was hilarious which was very unkind as you shouldn't mock the afflicted...

Cheesy fist

Penultimate class today! Reuben wasn't there so I had to make do with Pippa and Alfie the labradoodles and Rowley the setter. It was very, very hot and I struggled to find the energy or enthusiasm to do anything at all. We did walking round the others and learning to mind our own business, some "waits" with and without food, and some retrieving. Tarn the border was really impressive at this: he rushed out, picked up his toy and brought it straight back to his boss. I, on the other hand as the only true retriever in the class, went and picked up my toy and then dropped it before tootling back to Boss. (To be honest, I'm not very interested in toys unless Rosco is on the other end and of course, the best "toy" of all is Rosco himself). My favourite bit of today's class was when Lesley came up with a piece of cheese in her hand and I did my utmost to get it by biting and pawing her hand. Eventually, after a very long time I gave up and then magically her hand opened and I got the cheese! Why do I think Boss is not going to be repeating this exercise at home?

My first (and probably last) dog show – and rosette

Just around the corner from where we live is an old people's home and they held a fun dog show this afternoon. Boss is so not a dog show person – not interested in anything competitive in fact – but she thought it would be a good experience for me to meet lots of other dogs and people. I found it all a bit overwhelming and I completely forgot how to walk on the lead without pulling. A woman with a clapped-out collie suggested Boss got a skateboard so I could tow her. Boss was *not* amused. Just for fun, she entered me in the Coolest Pup class (well, I could hardly have entered Best Looking Lady or Veteran or Crossbreed or Most Obedient could I?) I didn't win but got a rosette just for entering and since it's red who's to know it's not a first? Boss was fascinated by the winning goldenoodle (a cross between a golden retriever and poodle) because she was so unlike a puppy: very unfriendly, no tail wag and much too quiet for her age in Boss's opinion. Boss says she'd rather have a pup with some life in it – which is lucky for me since nobody could ever accuse *me* of being lifeless! Plenty of time to be quiet and boring in the years ahead.

Mucky pups

When Boss heard that six month old English setter Rowley had never been off the lead because his bosses were worried he wouldn't come back, she offered to walk with them on the assumption that he would hang around with me. We met them beside the river and oh! what a lot of fun we had. We rolled in all the thick river mud and then jumped in the dyke where Rowley ducked me (I don't think he was really trying to drown me, he just didn't realise that because of my wonky legs I still can't swim) and then back into the sticky river mud. In no time at all, Rowley was the world's only English setter with a totally black face and I turned into a liver flatcoat! You might not know this but river mud is not like ordinary mud: not only does it smell to high heaven but it remains firmly glued to hair (in our case) or jeans (in Boss's case). Boss doesn't worry about things like that but I'm not so sure about Rowley's bosses. They looked a bit shocked that their immaculate boy had turned into something from a horror movie! But I do hope they let him walk with us again as we had such a terrific time even if we did end up a couple of very tired, mucky, smelly pups. And of course Rowley didn't run off...

School's out for summer!

Today was the last class of the course and it involved lots of sausages! We had to stop at some white saucer things pretending that it was a zebra crossing, then in and out of cones, round a tricycle and then wait before going through a gate. I did the gate waiting perfectly before but the heat addled my brain this time and I wandered off. Then we had to go through a tunnel. Despite Lesley, Liz and Boss doing their utmost to tempt me in with bits of sausage, I flatly refused – the only pup to do so. Rowley (smelling considerably sweeter than our last meeting) came to help persuade me through but no, I decided I didn't like it. Finally we had to find bits of sausage under flower pots which I thought was a great idea although I was just as happy to eat the flower pot. Most of us found the food by fluke, knocking or tripping over the pot, but Alfie the labradoodle had a terrific technique. He carefully lifted the pot off each bit of sausage! At the end I proved that I can remember what "wait" means: while Boss went to get a glass of squash I sat as good as gold, the only one to do so. Typical, of course, that Lesley didn't see such superb obedience!

Out of my depth

Boss is always up early and this morning was no exception but today she skipped her bath and by 6.30am we were on the beach. There, to my amazement, she stripped off and waded into the sea! I was a bit worried that she was going to disappear so I swam – or tried to – out to her. Boss says my attempts at swimming remind her of a pedalo: knees frantically going up and down like pistons making lots of noise and splashes but not going anywhere fast! She turned me round and pointed me back towards the beach. A few waves broke over my head but I didn't mind so I swam out to her again and again she pointed me landwards. Then I rolled and rolled in the sand until I looked like a little sand dog. Normally Boss won't let me swim in the sea because round here the beaches shelve very steeply and suddenly with powerful rip tides and she worries that I would get into trouble. But this is the one beach where you can safely walk out on sand; not surprisingly it's very popular so we didn't stay long be-cause even at 7am lots of other swimmers and their dogs were be-ginning to arrive.

Pavement pounding

The horrible heatwave is over – what a relief! – so Boss decided it was time to do some proper lead work. Living in the country, neither Rosco nor I are ever really on leads. I'm very good on the Common but not so impressive when there are loads of distractions. So Boss took me into town to walk up and down the high street. It was quite exciting: cars, a tractor, people, children, other dogs, prams, cycles and at first I was all over the place trying to say hello to everyone, earning myself a "Leave!" every few minutes. But after a bit I was exhausted and walked quite well beside Boss, learning to ignore people and stopping and sitting every time we crossed the road. We went into a shop for some bait (don't ask – sea fishing is apparently a treat in store for me and Rosco) and an old spaniel came up to say hello. I was very good and didn't try to pounce on him. Pounding the pavement and criss-crossing the road wasn't the most thrilling of excursions but something tells me we shall be doing it again and again until I walk nicely. But as the man in the bait shop said, "He's plenty of time to learn."

Rebellion

Another playdate with Reuben. As always we walked behind the beach at Dunwich, jumped in the stinky water and on each other and then went to The Ship for lunch. But I don't think we'll be going there again – or at least, not until winter. We always used to sit in the bar which was quiet and peaceful because children were ban- ished to the conservatory or garden. But they have decided to allow children in there now so it was full and very noisy. We sat in the garden but that too was packed with dogs on and off leads and children. Reuben and I thought it was great; Boss and Clare clearly didn't. So it will be pastures new inland next time. This morning Boss took both me and Rosco for a short walk and I decided it was time to show I have a mind of my own; after all, I am nearly six months old which means I can think and decide for myself. She whistled and, as usual, Goody Goody Four Paws went rushing back. I followed for a bit and then stopped. She whistled again and although I knew perfectly well what I was meant to do, I decided to ignore her so she turned and walked in the opposite direction. Eventually she got hold of me, made me sit and wait – which I did – and then called me in. Rosco just sat and watched with a look that said, "Why do you always have to make such a song and dance about everything and hold up our walk?" He seems to love doing what he's told but *I* don't!

It's official: I'm a boy!

At long last I have *cojones* – proof that I am a real full blooded male! A bit late, it's true, but better late than never. Boss is really relieved as she didn't want me castrated but if they hadn't appeared – or only one had dropped – she would have had no choice because of the risk of testicular cancer. So it's two cheers all round!

Introduction to pigs

I have had such an exciting day! First of all I met some pigs! We were walking along a track when I spotted lots of little pink animals with funny curly tails so I shot through the hedge and then a wire fence which gave me an odd tingle to take a closer look. I really wanted to play with what I have since learned were piglets but their mums were very big and the way they were looking at me was not exactly friendly. Besides, Boss was shrieking at me to come back so I decided perhaps another day and beat a retreat. Then we went fishing. While Boss messed around with the rod and some delicious smelling squid, Rosco and I played in the sea. On the way back Rosco spied a ball half way down the cliff and launched himself over the edge to retrieve it. (I don't how he does it but Rosco is an ace at finding other dogs' balls in brambles, bracken, woods so our garden is littered with his trophies). I was going to go too but Boss grabbed hold of me and stopped me. She says the two of us will be the death of her, what with pigs and cliffs...

A lifeline

Another playdate with Reuben. We walked beside the river which was lovely and cool. I am a true flatcoat because I spend more time in the water than out of it! Reuben and I played as always but at one point I must have accidentally hurt him because he turned on me. I was very taken aback. (Boss keeps telling me that I am very lucky that Rosco never tells me off, despite the fact that at times I must bite his ear a bit too hard because he yells). Anyway it wasn't serious with Reuben and we soon made up. Afterwards we had lunch in a new pub which was really friendly and no children but a little black dog that had a go at Reuben. Perhaps that was his just desserts for having a go at *me*! Boss has bought a long training line (says she's never had need of one before) but I showed her I could have saved her money because when I have it on, I return as soon as I'm called. Perfect puppy (on a string)! We've done more "swimming" in the sea. We go very early in the morning when nobody else is about. I'm still not very good so I don't go out as far as Rosco but I love the swell of the waves and when I get tired I just hang on to his tail for a free ride back. He's my lifeline!

First gundog lesson

This afternoon I had my first retrieving lesson. Earlier Boss had taken Rosco out on the Common with the game bag (this is a big bag she uses on shoots and Rosco goes nuts when he sees it stuffed with various dummies as well as the dummy launcher) for a refresher session. Then she came home and took me out with the long line and just a puppy dummy. She made me sit and then threw the dummy and said "Out!" I picked it up and brought it back to her and she didn't have to use the line to haul me in at all. We only did it a couple of times so that I didn't get bored.

Who needs sleep?

We met up with my setter friend Rowley for a lovely walk in the heather and bracken before going back to his place for a coffee and yet more fun. There was a big tank in the garden and I heard a splash. Whooooopppppeee *water*! I thought and jumped up for a closer look. There were all these great big fish in different colours and I was just about to leap in and join them when Boss grabbed me.

49

(Think if I'd made it into the tank it would have brought a beautiful friendship to a very speedy end!) Rowley and I had the greatest games racing round the garden and biting each other – we are perfectly matched in size, speed and personality – while his boss and mine tried to take pictures of us. Finally Boss and I went home where I romped with Rosco for a while and Boss kept saying "Why aren't you tired? You ought to be asleep!" I finally crashed out at 8pm – dead to the world as only a not-yet six month old pup can be.

Blessed Beau

Yesterday Boss took me and Rosco to an animal blessing service in Blythburgh church. It was so exciting: there were lots of dogs, a couple of cats and guinea pigs and three horses! Reuben and his housemate Polyanthus were there too. In the pew behind us there was a very shy lurcher and I was desperate to say hello to her but Boss kept a firm hold of me. Rosco fancied her too and his wagging tail made such a loud drumbeat on the pew that people were looking round and laughing. The vicar talked about a Staffie called Sergeant Stubby who was in the front line during the First World War and someone read the story of Balaam's Ass with a very lifelike donkey hee-haw! During the service each owner blessed their animals (I'd curled up and gone to sleep by that point) and then on the way out the vicar blessed each and every one of us in turn. Before the service Boss took us for a short walk by the river. I was all for diving in but Boss kept yelling "Beau NO!" although she was happy for me to jump in the dyke on the other side of the footpath. I am lucky in that Boss doesn't mind us wet and mucky but she says that until I am a better swimmer with sufficient brain to spot a flooded river, strong current or rough sea we will keep to shallow water or I have to be on the lead. Rosco loves the water too but he seems to know when it's dangerous and I will have to learn that too, in time.

Me and Rowley

Boss has a soft spot for Rowley because English setters are her second choice breed. She says when she is too old to cope with a mad flatcoat, she'll get a comparatively civilised setter! When we were all out the other day, she called me and I pretended I couldn't hear her. She called again and *Rowley* ran to her so *I* ran to his bosses. "Let's swap," said Boss – a little too enthusiastically, I thought.

Reuben's head first dive!

We met up with Clare and Reuben for a walk by the river and hoovering up of tasty cow pats. We stood on the bridge and Reuben looked a little too far over and fell in the water head first. Clare was a bit panicky but Reuben is a feisty little spaniel and a much better swimmer than me so he paddled under the bridge and pulled himself out the other side, none the worse for wear. Later, in the pub we were both told we were too old for playing games under the table now so I curled up and went fast asleep. And consequently missed out on biscuits from the landlady. So much for behaving....

So grown up

I am so grown up now that I spent a morning playing with Rowley at his house *on my own!* Boss has a pain in the neck (please note, I said *has*, not *is)* and had a physio appointment not a million miles from their house so Rowley's bosses suggested I went and played there. Boss was a bit worried: not about me but for their prized carp and beautiful flower beds. When she came to collect me she asked if I'd been concerned that she'd gone. Was she joking? I was far too busy playing to notice she wasn't there, let alone miss her!

Six months old today!

It's hard to believe that just four months ago I was so small I had to have my own water bowl on the floor as I couldn't reach the one on the stand. Now, I am nearly as tall as Rosco (and he's a big boy for a flatcoat) and just as handsome. The days when he couldn't stand me are long gone: now he's the very best friend and playmate any dog could have. The other day we met a woman with *eight* dogs and yes, they were all hers. I am so glad there are just the two of us. It means I have a companion but also a lot of Boss's attention. Every day she still has Rosco-time when she walks him for two to three hours and Beau-time when just the two of us do things together. If there were eight of us there wouldn't be enough hours in the day for such one-to-one attention!

Just the three of us

We had loads of fun with Bella, the golden retriever today. We went for a walk and then to a pub for lunch where the three of us sat patiently under the table in the shade. Or at least Rosco did, experience telling him that no titbits were going to come his way. I am young enough to live in eternal hope so I alternated between snoozing and sniffing. Bella though was all agog because her boss Barbara always gives her something from her plate. Boss does *not* approve! But she forgives her inevitable scrounging because there is no sweeter natured dog than Bella. I try to bite her and lick her but all she ever does is turn away – never a growl or lift of the lip. Boss says it's a pity she doesn't tell me off and then I might learn that not every dog is as even tempered as Bella and Rosco.

All the fun of the fete

Boss's reaction to August bank holidays is to batten down the hatches and not stir out on the roads. But she made an exception this year by taking me to the local fete cum dog show, partly to support the village and partly as a training exercise for me. (We left Rosco at home because he shares Boss's view of crowds). There were more dogs than I have ever seen, of every shape and size, plus hundreds of people, lots of noise and food everywhere – wow! Lots of people complimented me on my glossy coat and one woman actually asked Boss what she fed me. (For the record: kibble plus various extras like sardines, tripe, yogurt, fresh vegetables, scrambled egg, liver and fish). I met an 18 month old chocolate Labrador called Mogol who was as boisterous as me and some friendly lurchers. But some dogs were not so nice including a terrier called Muffin who went for me twice, the second time opening up my nose – and I really hadn't done anything to deserve it, like bounce on him. Boss says she is happy for a dog to warn me off as that is the only way I will learn to be less bumptious but not to really hurt me and draw blood. So we moved on to more congenial company which we found in the shape of Julian and Sophie. Sophie is a venerable old English setter and despite being well into her teens she is very sprightly and sociable; when I licked her nose she just waved her tail at such cheeky behaviour. Often dogs get snappy when they get old – like some humans – but not Sophie. Sunday was a sunny day so Boss took Rosco out for a bike ride and then spent the rest of the day gardening with my help. Rosco likes to sit in the shade by the back door where he can keep an eye on Boss as well as anyone approaching the gate but I like being close to Boss. So I sat in the shade of the wheelbarrow which meant every few minutes I had to get up as she moved it on. Today it's horrid and wet so Boss is going to do some dummy work with Rosco and then curl up in the armchair with me and her book.

Some people are so rude...

Today I went for my six month check up with vet nurse Vicki. She looked in my mouth and found all my baby teeth have gone, in my ears and eyes – and I inspected hers. Fair's fair! She also checked my feet and weighed me (a fraction under 23 kilos) and said I was spot on. And she thought that with luck the injury Muffin caused will fade without leaving a permanent reminder. While we were there Boss handed over my old puppy food for a local rescue centre and picked up the orthopaedic report from my X rays last month. I think she rather wished she hadn't as seeing it in black and white seemed to depress her a bit. Then we walked by the river with Reuben and

Clare. I jumped in and then struggled to get out so Boss ducked under the barbed wire to give me a hand. Unfortunately she snagged her mac on the wire so now has a big hole in her back. And as if that wasn't bad enough, I then jumped back into the river and got myself out – so she tore it for nothing. *Not* a popular puppy... In the pub afterwards lots of people made a big fuss of Reuben as usual. Clare is really nice and always points out that there *is* another puppy in the corner but they just glance over at me and then turn back to continue admiring Reuben. It's enough to make any chap feel a bit left out! Then, to add insult to injury, a man came up and asked what sort of "retriever cross" I was. When Boss said I was a pure-bred flatcoat, he grunted and said I didn't look like one and they were useless as gun dogs as they were loopy. I felt Boss bristle as she pointed out that her two previous flatcoats had been successful working gun dogs and that she hoped I'd be her third. But perhaps not, in the light of my wonky legs...

Soggy ears

While Boss had her head pulled about by the physiotherapist I had my ears tugged by Rowley. As soon as he saw me he gave me a big hug and no, he wasn't trying to hump me, this is just how he always greets me. We raced around the garden, pretending to be racehorses, chewed, sucked and chased each other until Boss came to collect me and it was time to go home. Having fun is *exhausting!*

Back to school – again

The start of a new term ... today I went back to school. There were some of my old friends there like Rowley, Pippa the labradoodle and Molly the cavapoo but not Reuben as he now goes to a different school. There were also lots of other puppies I'd not met before. There's a big boisterous boxer called Rosie, a funny little terrier, a completely mad chocolate Labrador and a Cavalier that "talks" a great deal. Our new exercises today were "stay" where Boss had to step away from me and then return, and "down" but without pointing at the ground to see if we actually understood the word rather than the gesture. Eventually I got the hang of this. Then we did the walk round the other dogs which I am awful at because I want to say hello to all of them so Lesley insisted Boss had a treat in her hand to keep my attention on her. I thought this was great but Boss wasn't very happy as it made me jump up and also, she argued, since she's trained all her dogs to walk nicely without pulling and never used a treat before, why do I have to be different? Then we did recall where Lesley's assistant Emma held each of us in turn and then, when released, we had to race back to our boss. Lesley laughed at my funny run – until Boss explained the reason. Then she told her how one of her dogs had had a dislocated toe pinned – considerably less complex than the knee and hip operations that possibly lie ahead for me – and how she wished she hadn't put her dog through it. I think hearing that made Boss feel a bit better as that's basically her point of view. Afterwards, Boss and Rowley's bosses David and

Paulette stood talking while the two of kissed and gently sucked each other. I got into trouble because a couple of times I leapt in the air and caught David first in one eye and then the other. He joked that I'd blinded him but Boss says it is absolutely not a joke and I *must* stop doing this.

Keeping cool

A walk by the river and lunch again with Clare and Reuben. I jumped in the river several times, quickly followed by Reuben. At one point I leapt up at Clare to give her a quick kiss but she didn't seem very impressed. This could be because I'd just emerged from the river and eaten a cow pat. We went to a different pub today and whereas I'm usually the one sound asleep and Reuben on the go, this time we reversed roles. Boss gave up trying to convert me into a well be-haved dog and let us play bite each other under the table. When we went in, Reuben was wet and stinky but by the time he'd cleaned himself on the walls, carpet and me, he left looking his usual golden self. Don't think we'll be going back there...

Plane crazy

Yesterday I went to my very first air show at Old Warden in Bedford-shire. It was the longest drive I've known so far (apart from the day I arrived, obviously) but I didn't mind because I had Rosco for com-pany in the back. There were lots of cars and people and quite a few dogs. We walked round before the show started and since I kept pulling on the lead, John walked with Rosco while Boss tried Lesley's trick of food in the hand. She must be joking! Why would I be interested in bits of sausage when there were people and dogs to meet and greet; steam engines, cars and aeroplanes to watch, to say nothing of bits of burgers and chips on the ground to eat? When the display started we sat down where there was shade for me and Rosco and I was very, very good (they both agreed) and slept a lot of the time. We fidgeted a bit when it got to our usual lunch time so Boss produced a picnic with gravy bones for us. John told us to "Watch the aeroplanes!" As if...! Once you've seen one, you've seen them all so I went back to sleep. The flying continued until nearly 7pm and we drove home in the moonlight: two plane crazy humans and two tired, happy and somewhat hungry dogs.

Introduction to a cat

At class today I proved just how contrary I can be! Lesley handed Boss some delicious sausage and cheese and of course with those in her hand I trotted along perfectly at heel – unlike on Sunday at the flying display. But the temptation of such delicacies soon wore off and I reverted to type, pulling towards the other dogs. When it came to the "stay" I was very good – although Lesley said I must not get up too quickly when Boss returns to my side. Rowley and I were both the best at this exercise – probably because we're the most laidback guys in class. Lesley said there is new research saying that dogs don't just like praise and titbits but really appreciate a good stroke and pat. Boss is certainly ahead on that one - she always makes a physical fuss of me when I do well. But she is also learning to say "Yes!" when I get it right rather than just "Good boy." After the class Rowley and I went for a walk. He kept grabbing me by the legs to try and make me play which I suppose is what I do to Rosco but never realised before how irritating it is when you're busy sniffing! On the way back we went to explore an open-plan garden, knocked on the front door but nobody seemed to be at home so, to our bosses' mortification (and yelling), we went round to the back door. Suddenly a cat leaped out which gave me a bit of a fright as I'd never seen one before. We were going to chase it but got grabbed by our collars in the nick of time which was lucky – for the cat.

Not just one but *two* handsome fellas

I think Boss and Clare are trying to work their way round every pub in Suffolk ... today we went for a deliciously muddy, stinky walk (Reuben turned into a very smart black and tan cocker) followed by lunch in Blythburgh. It was lucky it was such a sunny day that we could sit outside as the sight and smell of the two of us would have cleared the pub in seconds! As regular followers of my blog will know, it's usually Reuben who gets all the compliments when we go out together but today two really friendly waitresses thought that *I* was absolutely gorgeous and Reuben didn't get a look in. (Is that why Clare has suggested a different pub for next week???)

Brainy Beau

What a weekend! On Saturday we went to Bawdsey radar station, visited a round tower church, experienced live music, went on a pub crawl and swam in the river Deben. We also went for a short walk where I found the remains of a pheasant so I sat down and ate it.

Boss was appalled – apparently this is absolutely *not* appropriate behaviour for a potential gun dog! Then on Sunday we had a quieter day and Boss took us for a short walk in the evening to pick sloes. It's a funny place that I'd never been to before: you walk along a raised boardwalk because either side it's all wooded and boggy. Rosco raced off into the bog so naturally I followed him but by the time I regained the path I couldn't see either him or Boss. So I went back the way we'd come and sat by the car. A nice young couple on bikes came along and said hello and asked if I was lost. I thought of going off with them as they were obviously very kind and friendly but then I saw Boss and Rosco returning. She seemed somewhat panic-stricken – unlike me. Mind you, if I'd found the car had disappeared I would have been a bit worried but as long as it was there I knew they'd have to come back sooner or later. I'm not nearly as brainless as Boss thinks!

The Dogs' Guide to Suffolk Pubs

Another walk with Reuben but not a very successful one as it soon came to a road. Plus, I found the back end of a rabbit which I ate and Reuben decided that the field on the other side was more interesting than the footpath. *Another* pub... Reuben and I are becoming experts and plan to publish our findings on dog-friendly Suffolk inns! By the way, a few people have emailed to say that Rosco seems to be missing out on all the excitement. This is *not* the case! Believe me, Rosco has loads of fun walking on the beach or heath with Boss, going on bike rides as well as dummy training sessions in readiness for the start of the season next month. When I meet up with Reuben or Rowley this is Puppy-Only Time. Anyway Rosco doesn't like puppies because they jump in his face and he thinks there is nothing more boring than lying under a pub table for hours on end.

Say cheese

There weren't many of us in school today: my mate Rowley, Matilda the mad chocolate Labrador, Molly the cavapoo who spends most of her time on her back teasing us boys, Pippa the shy labradoodle, Rosie the boisterous boxer and Theo the King Charles who has to watch from the sidelines until he learns to shut up. We did some "stays" and I was really, really good and this time didn't get up when Boss returned to my side but stayed down. We did some "waits" when our bosses put a titbit in front of us but we were not allowed to touch it until told. Rowley made everyone laugh with this one: he did it the first time perfectly but the second time he threw himself down on the floor in disgust as if to say oh keep it, I don't care! He is a very expressive dog who leaves you in no doubt what he is thinking. We also did some recalls including one where assistant Emma called us for a piece of cheese and then we had to leave her and go back to our boss. Finally, some walking to heel. Boss held some cheese in her hand and I pranced up and down next to her – rather than pulling - which Lesley thought was a great improvement. Boss isn't quite so sure but she's prepared to give it a try rather than let me dislocate her shoulder. I think Lesley likes me. She said to Boss "You've got a really nice dog there."

Thank you Sheena

It was a bitter blow for Boss when she learned that I'd been born with bowed femurs; after all, we dogs are rear wheel drive and if I am to work all day as a gun dog, I need to keep the engine going! It's fortunate that Boss had never intended to either show or breed from me – because obviously neither is an option. Some people have suggested Boss re-home me but she says she won't even consider that – thank goodness – because buying a dog is like a marriage: for better or worse, for richer or poorer. It's just bad luck that I seem to be for worse and poorer! Since learning of the problem, the silence from my breeder has been deafening – certainly no offer of even a partial refund which many think there should have been – but in contrast, Rosco's breeder has been really helpful and supportive. It was Sheena who suggested that hydrotherapy might help me. Today was my first session at the hydro centre for assessment. Barbara is a fully qualified physiotherapist as well as hydrotherapist and she let me bounce about the room before putting me in a harness and showing Boss how to lead me forward and "brake" me. She also showed her how to stroke my legs, back and tail which was so relaxing I fell fast asleep. Boss was astoounded that something so apparently trivial could have such a dramatic effect. Barbara said that my back end is totally dysfunctional and that although I am not even seven months old, the muscles on my back legs are atrophying. This is why I can't swim! She aims to stop me using my front legs as compensation and to learn to move more normally and fluidly, using the back legs to drive me forward. So it will be a harness from now on, rather than collar and lead. When we return in a couple of weeks I am going to go in the pool with Barbara and an assistant, followed by what she calls land-based therapy. I think I'm really going to enjoy all this - so thank you Sheena!

Harnessed up

Following Barbara's advice, Boss ordered my Mekuti harness at 5pm on Friday and it arrived on Saturday morning! How impressive is that? What was not so impressive were Boss's attempts to fit it! In 40+ years of owning dogs she's never had one wear a harness so she fiddled around with it for ages until it looked like the picture in the leaflet. It feels a bit funny but I expect I'll get used to it. Boss then took me on the Common for a bit of training and for both of us to learn to walk with it. After that she dug out an old ramp and after walking along it on the grass and propped up against a tree stump, she tried persuading me to use it to get in the car. Which I did – with the aid of a few sausages! On Sunday we met up with old friends from the north for a pub lunch. There were four men at the next door table who made a big fuss of both me and Rosco. One of them laughed at my ears and asked Boss if she crimped them. (When they are wet they look a bit like unravelled knitting!) He told us he has a Staffie called Beau – but she is a bitch. Beau is a *boy's* name! It seems he didn't know that it was a traditional prefix for a fop or *man* of fashion like Beau Brummell and Beau Nash. Apparently lots of men in the southern American states are called Beau – after the famous Louisianan general in the American civil war. So it seems I am following in illustrious footsteps....

School work followed by fun

We all met up outside for this week's class and Lesley brought her Belgian shepherd over to say hello to me. I don't know who was the more surprised when he went for me; Lesley said he'd never done that before. We did some heelwork and recall which I was OK with, then we did what Lesley called the "finish" – ie I have to do a little circle behind Boss and end up next to her. Think this might need a bit more work – and a lot more sausage... Lesley wants us to learn some tricks which Boss is happy with as long as they don't hurt me – ie I won't be learning to walk on my back legs! Do you remember I told you how she taught me to shake a paw when I was very little? I think she's rather regretting that as I am now only too keen to wallop people with my big fat paws! She feels the "twist" is possibly a problem for my balance so we are going to learn the "roll over." Since I love lying upside down, this should be easy. Boss is still struggling to stop me leaping in the air at people so Lesley suggested that all visitors are armed with treats to throw to the ground. But Boss says that won't help unwitting strangers when we are out on walks and besides, she questions whether one should really get other people to train your dog! Rowley is even more unpopular than me with his leaping because he nips as well so he gets the water pistol treatment. I don't – because Boss thinks I'd love it! After the class we went for a short walk with Rowley and David and Paulette. I love walking and playing with Rowley because although we play bite each other, we never actually hurt. It was especially nice having fun with him this week as I have missed out on seeing Reuben. Boss and Clare planned to go out together in the evening so instead of the usual walk and pub lunch, they agreed to meet early in the morning with all four of us – ie me and Rosco, Reuben and Poly. But at the last minute Boss decided not to take me after all as she thought racing after three dogs might prove too much for my bent legs. I felt a little sad as I wondered whether this was a vision of the future: always being left behind and out of it as my friends grow bigger and capable of going further and faster than me.

Bang! Bang!

I went to a clay shooting club on Sunday for Boss to check whether I was happy with gunfire. She parked down the road where we could just hear the shots and then, since I showed no reaction at all, we walked into the ground. We got right up close to where there were six guns all firing at the same time. I'd like to say it was really exciting but, to be honest, I would have been bored to tears if it hadn't been for all the friendly people who came up to make a fuss of me and say hello to Boss. None of them could believe I was only seven months old: they thought I must be much older as I am such a big boy. We stayed for a while watching the shooting – or at least Boss did. I amused myself chewing a tree root. I may be lots of things but obviously I'm not gun shy!

How *not* to train the "down"!

I'm going to my first hydrotherapy session on Wednesday afternoon and as I'm not allowed to eat anything beforehand Lesley and Boss agreed it was a bit unfair to take me to class and see all the others getting titbits. Instead we went to an equivalent class last night. It was strange not seeing all my usual friends but there was a nice springador, a friendly Labrador, a very pretty husky and a miniature schnauzer who had come from another trainer that his boss wasn't happy with. We soon saw why! When we did the "down", the schnauzer's boss sat on the ground and pulled him under her leg, explaining that was how she had been taught! We all looked on in amazement but Lesley very kindly said "We do it a little differently here." She then showed her how to teach the "down" (ie a treat slid along the floor) while the rest of us did recalls. I have a tendency to stop short of Boss so Lesley showed her how to get me to come in really close by sitting on a chair with her legs apart. At the end of the class we did retrieving. Lesley gave me an old shoe to fetch which I raced over and picked up and took back – to Lesley! Well, it was *hers*. It wasn't the most brilliant display in the world but Boss doesn't seem too worried: it's early days yet.

Splish, splash!

I went for my first hydrotherapy session this afternoon. First of all Barbara and Clare put a little jacket on me and then led me through to the pool room. Clare showered me while Barbara held me and to start with I wriggled because I didn't like it. Then Barbara showed

Clare how to use her hand over me followed by the shower head and that made me stand very quietly. I think she might have done this before! Then I had to walk up a ramp to the pool. It looked a bit scary (could this really be me who usually leaps head first into any water?) but Barbara got into the pool while Clare held me and tempted me with a piece of cheese. Then Clare climbed in as well and they both held me to give me confidence. I tried drinking the pool but it was warm and tasted a bit odd so I washed both their faces instead. Meanwhile Boss was sitting at the end of the pool with a piece of cheese. The three of us moved across the pool to stand on an underwater pad – and I got the cheese. Then we all moved back to the other end back again to the pad. A piece of cheese didn't seem to be forthcoming this time so I sat down in the water, ever hopeful. Finally it was time to get out followed by another shower which I didn't mind this time, back into the first room for a towel-dry and then I was covered with a sort of blanket which I heard Barbara tell Boss was electro-magnetic therapy before I fell fast asleep. If this is water-based and land-based physiotherapy, I'm all for it! Obviously it can't straighten my bent bones but Barbara is hopeful that it will build up the muscles and teach me to walk better. She also thinks it will calm me down as she's a firm believer that movement and behaviour are interrelated. There is something about Barbara that is so restful and calming so is it the effect of her or the therapy? She was really pleased that I did so well today and says that Boss's gentle stroking at home is already making a difference. The good news is that she's happy for me to swim as much as I like in the sea, streams or our new pond (more of that another day); the bad news is that I can't go and play with Rowley tomorrow as planned because I need a day of rest after today's session.

V.E.P.

A few days ago Boss noticed that I have two deep symmetrical grooves on my front teeth so we went off to see vet Jenny. She said that my jaw is overshot but she didn't think it was so far over as to cause such damage. She was puzzled so she went and got the chief vet who agreed he'd never seen anything like it either. Had I been carrying iron bars, he enquired. Boss assured them that I had certainly not! So they took pictures and Jenny will send them off to a canine dentist for his view. We'll learn the verdict next week. So, another problem, another bill. Boss did a quick tally as to what I have cost her so far – and then wished she hadn't. The total expenditure in just seven months – excluding food and initial purchase but including classes, harness etc – comes to a mind boggling £949! I am a Very Expensive Puppy!

Pond life

Boss dropped me off at Rowley's for a couple of hours' fun this morning while she took Rosco for a wild, windy walk along the river. By the time she came to collect me, the kitchen floor was littered with every single toy from his toy box and the two of us were flat out with exhaustion. In the class last week that I had to miss, Rowley won a prize for his "twist." He showed it to us: no dog ever did such a stately, elegant rotation so his prize was very well deserved. Rosco and I now have our own personal swimming pool. Boss is suffering from the delusion that it is a wildlife pond, apparently in blissful ignorance that two flatcoats are the only sort of wildlife it is ever likely to see. I was the first in – in all fairness, by accident. I was standing on a slab on the edge leaning over for a drink when I toppled off and fell in head first. Since then I have tried to be helpful: it seems to have a lot of "weeds" in it so I have been busy pulling them out. What do you mean the plants were meant to be there?

Penultimate class

It was good to be back in my usual class this week although there were a couple of newcomers. One of the bosses had a King Charles but she used to have a flatcoat so she asked if she could make a fuss of me as she loves the breed. We went through everything we have learned (and supposedly practised): "stay", "finish", recall, walking on the lead. We did a 30 second stay but I would have happily stayed 30 minutes as this is my forte. We did two recalls where we had to run to Lesley for a treat and then to our boss for another. I did it very well the first time but on the second run I thought I'd just check that Lesley didn't have any other treats hidden on her as hers are a lot more exciting than Boss's. But overall I did OK and Boss seemed very pleased with me. Although Pippa and I had a few sneaky kisses under the chair and Rowley greeted me with his usual delighted hug when he arrived, we were all much better at sitting quietly and waiting our turn than we used to be.

I'm a puzzle!

The news from the dental expert about the strange marks on my teeth is that apparently they were just as puzzled as the vets! Their first thought was a traumatic injury caused by some sort of dental work but since Jenny assured them I hadn't had any, they think it has to be the result of something that happened very early on in my life before the enamel was formed so the exposure of the dentine has only now become apparent. If left alone, my teeth could become sensitive to cups of hot tea or cold ice cream but since they don't figure in my diet – sadly! – that is not a concern. More serious is that if left untreated, bacteria could leak into the tooth pulp leading to abscesses or dead teeth that would have to be removed later on. Before Boss makes any decisions one way or the other, Jenny is going to investigate further into exactly what the operation to fill the grooves with composite would involve. "I'm sorry you've got such a puzzling pup!" she laughed.

First shoot day

Now I know why Boss took me to the clay shoot to check I wasn't gun shy ... yesterday I went out on my first proper shoot! When we set off Rosco jumped into the back of the pick-up with five other dogs: black Labradors Rusty, Inca and Robbie, yellow Lab Jagger and springador Prince. Boss thought I'd cause havoc in there by jumping all over them so I sat on the back seat with her while Barry and Brian, the other picker-uppers, sat in the front. The fourth picker upper, Lee, and his three spaniels travelled separately from us towing the game cart. For the first drive we walked across a field and then sat for what seemed ages with nothing happening. (Boss says I will eventually realise that a lot of the time picker-uppers do absolutely nothing, unlike the beaters who are always on the go). Then lots of partridges burst out of the wood but despite a lot of bangs, none of them fell near us. So we walked on to the next drive where Rosco retrieved a partridge from a hedge. I was so keen to go and help him I nearly pulled Boss off her feet! She learned her lesson: after that I was tied to something immoveable for each drive like a tree or the quad bike or a giant screw if we were in the middle of a field. On the next few drives Rosco was back and forth retrieving pheasants and partridges having a whale of a time. At one point a partridge fell just a few feet from where I was tied up. I was dying to get it but no such luck: however hard I tried, I simply could not move that quad! Although I spent all day on the lead (some of the guns gave me funny looks as you don't usually see gundogs in harnesses), I really enjoyed myself. We didn't actually walk that far and I got lots of time to lie down during the drives and then back in our car at lunch time. I tried to say hello to some of the other dogs who seemed to think I was a bit of an upstart but eventually I managed to shut up and sit down nearby without pestering them. When I calm down I'll be allowed to ride in the back of the pick-up with the grown-ups.

Every dog deserves a delinquent day!

Today was the last puppy improvers class so what better day to play the fool! I spent more time upside down with my legs in the air than the right way up which got lots of laughs. After all, flatcoats are known as the clowns of the retriever world and don't forget, Boss plans an alternative future career for me as a comedian! I am normally an ace at the "stay" and will lie unmoving for ages but a new chap called Archie got up so I thought I'd just pop over and say hello. It's always nice to be friendly to newcomers. But Boss seems to understand that every dog has his off days and overall she is pretty pleased with my progress. To sum up... Notwithstanding the Archies of this world I am good at staying and waiting and I stop dead on the stop whistle. My recall is good until I get about six feet from Boss when I hesitate because I have a sneaky feeling that she is going to put me on the lead and I don't want the freedom to come to an end. And my heelwork still leaves a lot to be desired if there are distractions in the form of any other dogs about. Boss thinks we're both learning lots so she has signed us up to continue the classes which I'm really pleased about because they are the highlight of my week. And it's not just because of the treats that issue from food dispenser Lesley!

Kennel cough

No, not me, paws crossed, but Rowley. Perhaps because he was vaccinated against it (unlike me), his symptoms are not too severe but it still means that he is going to be out of circulation for a while as it is so contagious. The mystery is how and where did he get it? The only dogs he comes into contact with are me and those in the class. His vet suggested that he caught it from foxes – but maybe it was a mis-diagnosis and he doesn't have it at all? Poor Rowley. I hope he gets better soon.

Shoot days

Rosco and I went out on the shoot on Saturday and again yesterday. I don't like to tell tales but on the Saturday Rosco completely lost the plot and ran all over the place picking up and then dropping the birds! But he redeemed himself yesterday when he found a pheasant deep in a thicket that the other dogs had missed and caught up with two super-charged running partridges. One of them was so far away that I thought my best friend had gone for good. I am getting used to being screwed into the ground although I do whinge a bit when Boss and Rosco disappear in search of a pricked bird. But since she ignores me I soon realise I might as well shut up and just hope she doesn't forget to come back for me. Yesterday one of the guns very kindly unscrewed me and led me back to the trailer. Usually I have to stay on the lead all day but if Boss is stumbling through brambles she lets me off which is great!

Good and bad – in parts

In class today I did a really good "stay" and recall but then forgot about waiting before going through the gate and tried to say hello to everyone when we did the walk round the others. So, 50-50. To Boss's amazement Lesley said she thought I'd be up to doing the bronze test in two or three weeks. Not bad since I only turned eight months old yesterday. Boss isn't remotely interested in tests or certificates; she says all she wants is that I learn not to be in a pain in the neck to others (or pain in the shoulder to her) and enjoy life. I certainly do that and there is always lots of laughter at our classes. If I turn out to be a gun dog, that will be a bonus.

Cool in the pool

Today was my second session in the pool. Barbara is really pleased with me and says she can already see a difference in my movement although there is still a lot of work to be done. She says she wishes she had videoed my first visit when I was all over the place; now I am very calm, confident and well behaved (Barbara's words, not Boss's!).

A hard act to follow

A year ago today my predecessor died. From all accounts, Titus was an unforgettable flatcoat who lived life to the full. He was a gun dog with a great nose but with his own distinctive way of working. He loved going fishing with Boss and it was often a toss-up who got the fish off the hook first but he also caught a golden carp and trout all by himself. He was bilingual: in Spain he used to play with a neighbour's child who spoke not a word of English so he had no choice but to learn Spanish. He and Pablo spent hours playing hide and seek and bullfights (Titus was the *toro* to Pablo's *matador*). As a qualified Pets As Therapy dog he brought a huge amount of happiness to terminally ill children at a respite centre. He would sit on their beds, climb the steps to their Wendy house, perform endless rollovers on command and submit to the tightest bear hugs. He loved everybody and everything and was Rosco's beloved protector and playmate. (After his death Rosco went grey round his muzzle almost overnight). Titus is buried here in the garden; his grave is topped with a rose appropriately called Braveheart and smothered with forget-me-nots. Of course the reason I am here is because of the family link to Titus. Whether I follow in his pawprints and prove to be a chip off the old block remains to be seen....

So that's what it's all about!

I showed my potential as a gun dog on Saturday when we were walking back after a drive and I sniffed out a pheasant in the ditch. I was so excited I nearly dragged Boss with me into the hedge! But once I'd pointed it out Rosco went after it and got all the glory which was a bit unfair since it was *me* who found it. Boss asked Lee to hold me while she got the bird from Rosco and he commented on how strong I am. That was proved a bit later when Boss and Rosco went off to find a couple of birds in the woods. Moments later I shot past her, dragging the screw behind me! I have finally worked out what is happening on these shoot days. I used to think the dogs were just running around having a ball but now I understand they are looking for birds. I'm dying to help but it seems there's no chance this season. Maybe next year? In an ideal world I would not even be out on a shoot at eight months old but Boss can't leave me home alone all day and although there have been a few puppy sitting offers, she feels it is too much of an imposition on a regular basis. Besides, a whole day with me would probably stretch any friendship to its absolute limits! This time we stopped for lunch quite late and so afterwards Boss just took Rosco and left me sleeping in the car.

Moved up

Lesley emailed Boss to say she thought I was ready to move up a class. Rather rudely Boss thinks the move is because the other class is filling up rather than due to my brilliance. It was strange not seeing all my old friends in the new class; just Rosie the boxer was there. It was a bit daunting too because lots of the other dogs were really good and some of the other bosses looked a bit sniffy as I bounced around (Lesley calls me Tigger) but they are all much older than me. We did some exercises like going to sit on a bed. Boss threw a piece of cheese on it and I had to go and get it and then sit down. Easy peasy! I also had to come in really close between Boss's knees as she sat on a chair. We did the "finish" (not very good at this as we haven't practised it at all), walking to heel (I was great because Boss was cheating with some liver in her hand) and "stays" which as you know are normally my strength but this time everyone left their dogs and walked all the way round and I must admit I got up to say hello when the others came past me. I can't help it if I am so friendly! (Actually I think it's a reaction to my seriously anti-social Boss who spends ages planning walks where we will meet nobody). Then the advanced dogs did a funny sort of twist which I know Boss won't let me learn because of my legs. In the evening we went to the vet –

just for a change. I've had a funny lump on the back of one of my front legs for a while now and although it doesn't worry me in the slightest it has recently got a bit bigger with a funny dent in the middle. All the "vet checks" we do at class came in handy as I helped Jenny examine it by cleaning out her ears until I discovered something delicious in the bin. (Apparently it was methadone so obviously I have a future as a junkie!). Jenny thinks it's a benign tumour which is very common in flatcoats so she has given Boss some steroid cream to put on it. If it makes no difference in a week, then the lump will have to be taken off and sent away. While we were there, Boss asked Jenny to look at my dew claws which grow outwards instead of neatly down the leg as they do in Rosco. This means they could catch on things and rip out. And they also discussed my teeth. Jenny is having difficulty in obtaining the stuff to fill my grooves in small quantities (clearly not a lot of local dogs have fillings!) so she is waiting for quotes from canine dentists in Cambridge and Northampton and also, to find out what the likelihood is that bacteria will get into the dentine and rot my teeth. As the medical bills multiply, I am definitely Boss's little bundle of joy.

Lunch with Reuben

We met up with Reuben today – the first time for ages. Unlike me, he doesn't seem to have grown much – just acts a bit more grown up. We walked by the river and I had loads of fun rolling in bits of dead animals so I smelt absolutely delectable by the end of the walk. Then we went to the pub where we both behaved impeccably – well, apart from Reuben having a quick look to see if there was anything he fancied on the table before Clare yanked him off!

Appearances can be deceptive!

There I was, good as gold, motionless in the middle of the rape while Boss and Rosco searched for a bird. "Goodness, that puppy is good – sitting all by himself!" exclaimed one of the guns. "He hasn't any choice," laughed Boss, "he's screwed into the ground!" Sometimes Boss is just too honest for her own (and my) good. Usually on Sundays Boss takes Rosco out with the bike but today it was so windy she thought she might blow off so instead she took us both to the beach. There were really big waves which worried Boss as I kept paddling in and trying to drink the water. I still haven't worked out why the sea tastes funny. We met a man we often meet there but instead of his usual collie companion he had his other dog with him. Charlie and I had a tremendous game although I kept ending up sprawled in the sand. I know I'm lucky in that Rosco is nearly always happy to play with me but it is nice to have another playmate sometimes. Reuben doesn't seem to want to play nowadays but the good news is that Rowley will be back in circulation this week. He and I are twins as far as size and temperament are concerned. Both Rosco and I were in the doghouse this morning. Boss came downstairs and was decidedly not amused to find a dead rabbit on the dining room carpet. I was sitting - the picture of innocence – in my bed while Rosco was hovering by the back door, looking worried. Rosco has never taken a rabbit indoors before so Boss immediately jumped to the conclusion that *I* was the culprit. But it could have been worse – at least I hadn't eaten it all over the carpet...

Missing Bella

Looking at the rain today it's hard to believe what a lovely day we had yesterday in blazing sunshine. First, Boss walked us along the sea wall which we had all to ourselves apart from some cows in a field. (Since there was only a dyke between us and them Boss put me on the lead). Then we met up with Boss's friend Barbara but sadly no Bella because she has become paranoid about getting in the car. Despite the fact that it's November it was really warm and we sat outside the pub but because I had tried to drink the North Sea dry I was terribly thirsty. It took Boss a while to realise why I was fidgeting (sometimes her communication skills are seriously lacking) but once the penny dropped she brought me two enormous bowls of water. I drank and drank and drank and then, inevitably, I peed and peed and peed, nearly flooding the river Deben in the process. Finally we all went for a lovely walk in the sunshine. A perfect day ... shame that Bella missed it.

Five steps forward, five back

We learned lots of new things in class today. The others are all twisting but Boss won't let me do that. She did try to teach me (with Lesley's help) the "fold." Here I have to go down but not in the normal way – ie forwards – but backwards on to my haunches. Not sure the two of us are going to grasp this; besides Boss is wondering not only what the point is but also whether my deformed legs should be doing such a movement. We did some "stays" and I was very good at staying put and then some walking to heel, off lead. Now this *is* something Boss and I have been practising while we are out on walks and although I say it myself, I'm pretty ace at it – when there are no distractions. Class, of course, is different! When we set off I tried to pop over to see another dog but after a reminder from Boss of where I was supposed to be, I then kept by her side. So far, so good but just imagine how boring it would be if I were perfect all the time. Not so long ago I was good at the "stop" whistle and waiting until Boss caught up with me but now, although I stop for a moment, I can't be bothered to wait. I worry that she's going to put me on the lead and spoil everything. The other day I was very naughty and ignored her totally, skipping round the gate so that I ended up on the road. Luckily nothing was coming – apart from a very cross Boss. So I go back as much as I go forward. After class Boss took me and Rosco for a lovely walk by the river. I met some swans for the first time but even I was a bit frightened when they hissed at me and eventually decided – just for once – that discretion was the better part of valour.

Busy – but nothing exciting

Saturday was a shoot day and a bit over-dogged so there wasn't a lot for Rosco to do. I am now very good at sitting quietly during the drive but when Rosco goes after a bird I desperately want to go too and jump up and down and pull like crazy. On Sunday we had a wild, wet walk on the heath and then a lovely cosy afternoon in front of the fire. Boss had to go to the dentist in Southwold yesterday which meant a different walk along the river bank there. There were some cows just the other side of the reeds but Boss was adamant: I may *not* go and say hello. Today we met up with Reuben on the beach and Rosco came too. We met a young lurcher who was very keen to play but he was so fast I couldn't keep up with him! Reuben found a gull's wing which Clare made him leave. I went and picked it up instead and a furious Reuben really laid into me. Boss had to pull him off. Rosco and I are so used to taking things off each other that it never occurred to me that he would mind and to say I was a bit surprised at his reaction is an understatement. When we were nearly back by the cars, he vanished into someone's garden and refused to come back. Clare was very, very cross with him. It is heart warming to see someone else being told off for a change!

A head start on the down

My wonky legs mean it's much more comfortable to lie down rather than sit which gives me a terrific head start in class when it comes to the "down" – because I'm already there! Boss and Lesley have agreed that not only should I not do the "twist" but also the "fold." So when the others do that, I do down in the normal forwards way. Today we did the recall and Lesley reminded Boss that I am less likely to stop a foot away if she stands up straight, two minute "stays" (I never moved), and off-lead heel work round another dog. We also swapped dogs: terrier Harley really wanted her boss rather than mine but you know me, I'm always happy whatever so I just lay on my back with my legs in the air.

Out of the window – into the melee

We were picking up two days running this week. On the Friday Boss decided to leave me in the pick-up for one drive because she and Rosco were standing nearby and she could see what I was up to. First, I sat on the back seat and then got in the front behind the steering wheel. But when the shooting started I got very excited, lent on the slightly ajar window and it went all the way down! So out I jumped...oh, what fun! I raced around after Rosco and then found Barry and his dogs. Barry thought I was Rosco so was totally unprepared when I leapt on him with huge enthusiasm. He's not a very large man so I nearly sent him flying! As a result, on the Saturday I graduated to sitting in the back of the pick-up with all the other dogs: Rosco, Labradors Jagger, Inca and Rusty and springador Prince. I was very well behaved and didn't jump all over them as Boss had feared but I got left behind on most of the drives although I did have Jagger's company for one because she was limping.

Absence makes the heart grow even fonder

At long, long last we met up with Rowley for a walk. It seems like ages because of his alleged kennel cough. We had the kind of terrific time only best friends can enjoy: jumping over and on each other, biting legs, pulling ears, sending the other flying in the mud etc. I did my utmost to lead him astray into the bracken and bushes and water but he's a bit shyer than me, to Paulette's relief. (Give me time and

I'll soon change that!). We walked for quite a long time so Boss thought I'd just go fast asleep when she later went out with Rosco. Not a chance. I was so bored I thought I'd see what was on television. No matter how hard I pressed the buttons with my teeth I simply could not get the remote control to work – not even when I removed the batteries. For some strange reason Boss didn't seem very happy when she returned...

Oh Boss how *could* you make me look so silly!

The first time I went to hydrotherapy Barbara suggested Boss buy me a coat so that I didn't catch a chill afterwards. Boss let the advice drift over her head – and again on the second visit. But the third time she agreed as the weather is getting colder and so I have ended up looking a right wally in a coat that dwarfs me (I think Boss thought she was measuring a wolfhound). I hope none of my friends see me in it: I'd die of embarrassment. Barbara was delighted with me today saying that she could see a great improvement in all my movement but especially my back legs. And Boss was thrilled because for the first time I swam properly with my front legs below the surface and using my back legs to propel me forward. OK, I did have a bit of help from Barbara and Sarah but I'm getting there ... I'll make the Olympics yet, you'll see. Sadly I won't be going back again until the new year because of my upcoming operation and then Christmas. I did well too in class this morning. I sat out while the others did reverses and "folds" and "twists" but I was good at the "waits", the two minute "stay" and even a "meet and greet" session with a new springer/collie cross called Reuben (another one!) and a chocolate Labrador called Elsie. And when Lesley came round to say hello to each dog I stayed sitting - possibly because Boss threatened to chop my legs off if I jumped up to grab her hair as usual! I must have been inspired by a super card Boss's friend Pat sent me showing a puppy snoozing in a deckchair and the words "Fetch, Heel, Sit, Stay ... Life is so complicated!" She says she saw it and immediately thought of me knowing I would appreciate the joke.

Beachcomber

We were meant to be meeting Clare and Reuben for a walk and lunch today but at the last minute they couldn't make it. Instead, just the three of us had a brilliant walk by the sea. We are so lucky living just a few miles from the beaches because there are always lots of interesting things to find: plastic bottles, rope, net, balloons and today we found a dead guillemot that had been caught with a fisherman's hook. And of course there are seagulls to try and catch and, when it is rough and windy, tiny flecks of foam to chase over the pebbles. Then I spent the afternoon helping Boss cook. I don't know what she'd do without me. I sit by the oven checking the temperature, I pick up things she drops and by wafting my nose along the edge of the work surface I double check she has all the right ingredients. I am nine months old today.

Keep your distance!

We were picking up both Friday and Saturday. On one drive I was tied to the trailer with Boss and Rosco just in front of me when a woman who was watching came over to me. "Don't get too close to him," warned Boss, "or he'll jump all over you." How mean of her! I was only going to say hello in my inimitable, irrepressible way. On the Saturday Boss was going to put me back in the car for the last drive when a very nice man called William offered to take me with him. He usually shoots himself but that day he was just watching. So Boss and Rosco disappeared into the woods and William and I had a ringside view of all the shooting. I was very good and sat quietly by his side and then, rather than hang around for Boss, the two of us set off back to the yard. "He's pretty strong isn't he?" commented William, rubbing his arm, as he finally handed me back.

I've been stitched up!

I knew there was something up this morning: Boss got up as usual, let us outside as usual, made a cup of coffee for herself as usual and went back upstairs as usual. What about our breakfast? Rosco and I looked at each other: dementia or something more sinister? As Boss and I walked into the vet, the penny dropped. Here we go again. Nurse Vicky weighed me (28.3 kilos) and tried to give me a pre med but I really didn't like it and wriggled so much that she had to get Jenny to help. Then I lay down and Boss stroked and talked to me as I got very sleepy. I was a little wobbly as Jenny and Vicky led me away but Boss promised she'd be there for me when it was all over. The good news is that Jenny had a close look at my deformed dew claws and decided not to remove them as the quicks are so far down, the nails can be trimmed really close. (I am *such* a disaster area: mis-shapen back legs, dew claws that grow outwards, grooved teeth and a horrible lump – which is why I was there, this time around). After about an hour I woke up and Vicky led me, a bit unsteadily back to Boss who was patiently waiting for me in reception and the two of them lifted me into the car. Once we were home Boss lit the fire, laid me down on my bed with a blanket over me and I slept soundly. Now and then I opened my eyes, saw Boss sitting there reading, so closed them and went back to sleep. When I woke up properly I realised I had a red bandage on my front leg which I tried chewing to see if it would come off. Boss said if I kept on doing that I would have to wear a great big lampshade on my head. It was difficult and painful to walk but Boss distracted me with some chicken and rice. Rosco keeps sniffing around as if to say "What's the matter with you, why are you just lying around?" At the moment I feel a little sore, sleepy and sorry for myself so I am going to say goodbye for now and climb on to the sofa for a cuddle.

Red leg

Believe me, I am not one of life's whingers (remember, I didn't even cry my first night away from my mum) but I did cry quite a bit last night because my leg hurt and I just didn't understand what was going on. But today it feels a little better so I'm a lot happier. And as Boss pointed out, if Jenny had removed the dew claws, I'd have *two* bandaged legs. I think Rosco thinks it's his Christmas stocking because he keeps sniffing and pawing it! This morning Boss took Rosco for a walk on the beach leaving me with a peanut butter-filled kong –

it took a little while to get used to the funny taste – in the hope that it would distract me from trying to undo the bandage. Then we spent the rest of the day sitting quietly in front of the fire.

Good news – at last!

I went back to the vet this afternoon to have the wound checked. Vicky listened to my heart and took my temperature and then wielded a pair of very sharp scissors. Jenny held on tight to me while Boss waved titbits in front of my nose and bingo! my stitched leg was laid bare. Jenny seemed pleased with her handiwork although it's a little inflamed at the bottom (little does she know the games Rosco and I have been playing!) but after some discussion they decided to put on another bandage, albeit slightly smaller and green this time. They sprayed it with bitter apple which is meant to put me off chewing it but actually I quite like the taste! The results from the biopsy are back and it is brilliant news. I have a histiocytoma which to you and me means that the lump is benign. There, in black and white, it says "the prognosis is good." Boss was over the moon with relief. Now she only has my teeth and legs to worry about... In the morning Boss took me to class, partly to give me a change of scene and partly as a less energetic way of passing an hour than playing with Rosco. I watched for most of it because they were doing things like jumping but I joined in for some off lead heelwork. One thing the others did was learning to stop and sit when their boss raised their hand but I already do that on the whistle (well, sometimes!). I don't think Lesley realises just how advanced I am. While we were there Boss bought me a squeaky donkey and so when we got home Rosco and I had a game of tug of war.

Just what the vet ordered .... not!

To stop me climbing the walls with boredom we have been going out for pub lunches where all I have to do is sit under the table and hope that someone notices me – which they usually do. Boss carefully timed my operation so that I would have a full 10 days of quiet to recover before going on the shoot again. Then Andrew rang to say he'd put on an extra day and inviting her to pick up. After a brief hesitation, she said yes, reasoning that sitting in the pick-up was probably more peaceful than playing with Rosco at home. It was a lovely day – small, informal and friendly with a mixture of beaters and syndicate guns shooting. Boss put me on the back seat of the pick-up to protect my bandaged leg and at times it was a bit of a squeeze but nobody complained – except Mr Grumpy but then he is always having a moan at somebody about something or other. Some humans are just born to be misery guts. Apart from him, it was a great day although my leg is a little sore today.

Fed up

Yesterday Boss took me back to the vet because my leg was so sore I was hopping about on the other three, my paw was so swollen it looked like a lion's and the wound was weeping. Jenny cleaned it up and decided it would be better without the bandage but I was on no account to lick or chew at the stitches. This means that when Boss isn't there – like all night – I have to wear the ridiculous lampshade.

It bangs into things and makes it almost impossible to eat my marrow bone. Rosco comes and looks inside it as if to say "Whatever are you wearing that silly thing for?" I shall be so relieved when the stitches come out and I can go for walks again and play with Rosco and Rowley. In the meantime, I am thoroughly fed up...

Unstitched but re-bandaged!

Thanks to my leg, training has been on the back burner so it was a bit of a shock to go back to class today and be expected to behave. No concessions for post-op patients! But I did go through the tunnel this time (you remember how I flatly refused last time?). We did "bed" and "stays" in the normal way and we also had to stay when someone else's boss walked round us. Because my leg was quite sore, I was very happy not to move. In the afternoon we went back to Jenny to have the stitches out – well, those that I hadn't helpfully taken out myself. (I've been very good at wearing the lampshade but because I am a natural contortionist I have managed to scratch my leg with my back foot! Pretty clever, huh?). Boss thinks the wound looks disgusting – she's very squeamish about things like that – but Jenny didn't seem too bothered. She squeezed some cream on it and bandaged it up again – first red, then green and now I have a white one. (Don't think it'll be white for long!). When Boss isn't around I still have to wear the lampshade which I really hate because it crashes into everything including Rosco who gets upset and runs away and then won't play with me.

Two days out

Vet Jenny was happy for me to go to the shoot on Friday and Saturday providing I didn't leap about with the other dogs and damage my healing leg. Boss was a bit worried about this but as it turned out, Rosco and I had the pick-up all to ourselves because Brian and Lee weren't there and Barry was on the quad. It was so wet and muddy everywhere that Boss decided I was best out of it which meant I missed all the excitement but at least I had Rosco to keep me company in between drives. After lunch there was just one drive so Boss left me in the car with my kong which kept me amused until I fell fast asleep. By the end of the second day I think Rosco was feeling his age. After picking over 100 birds, all he wanted to do was curl up in his corner of the sofa and go to sleep whereas I was still bouncing. Boss played with me for a while until I too crashed out and dreamed of the day when *I* am going to retrieve hundreds of birds.

Slow but sure

Back to the vet – again! Jenny is confident the wound is healing, albeit slowly. It's taking such a long time because it's in an awkward place on my leg, under constant pressure. She wants the air to get to it at night so I have to wear the lampshade but not the bandage, but during the day it has to be wrapped up. The good news is that I am allowed to go for walks again as long as they are not wet and muddy. This is *not* easy – unless we walk up and down the A12! But at least it means I can meet up with Rowley again.

Party time

This was my very first party and goodness, was it exciting! Lesley combined two or three of her training classes so there must have been at least 20 dogs there of varying ages and sizes. Quite apart from the Christmas music blaring out, the noise was amazing – as you can probably imagine. Sadly I missed the first game as my bandage slid down to my ankle – Boss may have several skills but bandaging is not amongst them – so she had to hurriedly improvise. But then we played musical mats and we actually got into the final only to be eliminated because Boss, rather than me this time, had to sit on the mat and she was too slow. (This is an instance when it's a distinct advantage to have a young, fit owner...). We played a relay race where I had to jump a little pole, weave in and out of plates of sausages, go through a tunnel, pick up a Father Christmas hat and then back again. I went through the tunnel without hesitation and no liver bribes! For another game we had to stay while our bosses built a tower of biscuits just in front of us and I won a prize for this because I wasn't tempted into budging an inch. I'm very chuffed with my prize because it's a stretchy toy that Boss had been contemplating buying me when she chose the squeaky donkey instead the other week – so now I have both. Once all the games were over the bosses ate sandwiches and sausage rolls and cake while boxes of dog biscuits were passed round for the real guests. Boss said it was quite the noisiest and most exhausting party she'd ever been to but I loved it!

Out again

Since my operation just over two weeks ago, the only times I've left the house have been to go to the vet, school and the pub. So today it was brilliant to actually go out for a walk and what made it even better was meeting up with Rowley. We had loads of fun chasing, leaping over and pouncing on each other. We didn't walk very far but unaccustomed as I have become to so much running around I was quite tired afterwards and happy to go to sleep in my lampshade while Boss walked Rosco.

Dog on the loose

Yesterday Boss took me and Rosco to the heath for a walk because it is relatively dry underpaw there. We raced through the bracken and round the trees – magic! I've heard that some dogs are never allowed off the lead which I think is really sad as there is nothing to beat running free with the wind in your hair and exotic smells in your nostrils. In the afternoon we went back to the vet. Jenny says I no longer have to wear the bandage or the lampshade (providing I keep my tongue in my mouth) but Boss has to apply cream to the wound twice a day. We have to go back again so I am not signed off yet. Today we went out on the shoot but it was a smaller day than usual which meant we didn't stop for lunch so I didn't get out of the pickup at all. Well, apart from the one time I leapt out and escaped for a couple of minutes. I went to say hello to a little Jack Russell called Cynthia (yes, really!) who snapped at me, giving Boss a chance to grab me and put me back.

Getting in the Christmas spirit

This will be my very first Christmas but Boss says I have been so full of beans the last few days, anyone would think I know what is coming. I have eaten six Christmas cards; opened a present that was obviously not for me (soap – yuk!); nicked some carrots and parsnips off the vegetable rack; chewed the bag the venison came in, in the hope that there might have been a bit left in it (there wasn't), and swiped an empty chocolate box off the table. This morning Rosco and I raced along the beach where we met the collie we often see there and my leg got a good salt wash as I paddled in the sea. Then we spent the afternoon tearing around the garden playing tug of war; although I am six kilos lighter than Rosco I can pull *him* now! Then it was time to see vet Jenny who is happy with my leg although I still have to have it creamed and go back to see her in a week. I can't think why some dogs don't like going to the vet. I *love* it! Linda, Carina and Molly always come round the counter and make a fuss of me and Jenny is oh-so-gentle and as long as I don't chew her stethoscope is happy for me to clean her face while she examines me. She and Boss chatted about dogs that end up spending their Christmas at the vet because they have eaten stuff like mince pies, Christmas pudding, chocolates or stuffing. Even fatty gravy can cause pancreatitis. Jenny is on duty over Christmas so she said, much as she loves me, she hopes she is *not* going to be seeing me! I should be so lucky: I was disappointed to hear Boss tell her that Rosco and I wouldn't be getting anything special at all; the greedy pigs are going to eat all that venison themselves. Happy Christmas everyone.

My first Christmas

Eight o'clock in the morning found us on the beach but others had had the same idea so Boss decided to take us on the heath instead. There we came across two huge black dogs and some sort of terrier. Luckily they were on the leads as they were all snarling and snapping. Rosco took one look and walked off but I thought this was a novel way of playing so I pranced around them, play bowing. Boss hauled me away, warning me that if I didn't realise that when dogs shows their teeth they mean business, I am going to come a cropper. But I don't understand: why would anyone want to hurt *me*? Then home for pressies. Our friend Bella had given us each a bag of liver bites. I tried to get both of them in my mouth; it's not that I'm greedy you understand, just that Rosco is so laidback (or lazy). I did all the hard work of ripping off the paper while he just watched and then Boss made me share the contents with him. Then Boss gave us hers: Doris the donkey who makes a funny groan rather than a squeak and a monkey rope. Sadly Doris didn't last very long. I don't think she was designed for tug of war and so now she has been taken away for major surgery. We spent most of the day racing around the garden with a selection of toys until finally it was time to curl up in front of the fire and sleep. I wish it could be Christmas *every* day!

Beau the Bold

Boss is worried that I am totally fearless: rabid dogs, frisky horses, hoof-kicking heifers, threatening pigs, you name it – not much scares *me*! (Except when Rosco barks at someone at the gate and then I rush indoors and look out of the window). Boss says it's fine to be confident but it needs to be tempered with caution for survival. But on Sunday morning, walking early in the forest, even I was intimidated when a team of huskies towing a quad bike came hurtling round the corner. Boss whistled and Rosco ran to her and, after a moment's deliberation so did I. The man halted the team while Boss put our leads on but I don't think he'd have managed to hold them for long because they were howling and leaping up and down in the traces, impatient to get going again. As they swept past us, I was happy to watch from the safety of the trees. The good news for the end of the year is that Jenny has finally signed off my leg. No more cream – we just have to wait for the scabby bits to fall off. But we shall see her again next week anyway when I go to get my passport. How exciting is that!

Resolutions

Today is the start of a new year when apparently everyone makes promises that they break within weeks. Boss has drawn up a daunting list of resolutions for me...

1. I will stop mugging friends and innocent strangers because I have to understand that not everyone loves me - hard as

that is to believe. (And that some people prefer to go to the loo unaccompanied).

2. I will not poke my nose where it's not wanted: in the cupboards, tumble drier, fridge, empty wine bottles, wood shed and so on. And if I persist in going into the utility room Boss will leave me there, knowing I can't open the door from the inside.

3. We have lots of mice holes in the lawn and one of my pleasures is sniffing out the occupants and then trying to dig them out. But I'm to understand that a lunar landscape is *not* an attractive feature in a garden.

4. I will stop pulling on the lead not least because Boss says that until I do, we will do endless lead work every day. (This is what is known as boring me into submission).

5. I will learn that not all dogs want to play with me or be bounced on and understand that when they show their teeth they are *not* grinning and that it is time for me to beat a retreat.

6. The recall whistle is *not* optional. I must return at once even if I am having fun playing with another dog or in hot pursuit of something.

7. I will not remove the few remaining plants in the pond nor pick the roses.

8. I have plenty of toys of my own so it is not necessary to pinch things that don't belong to me and then leave them out in the rain –like Boss's brand new sheepskin slippers.

Phew!

That was the week that was...

We met up with Rowley and had a terrific time chasing each other through the woods. It's great with Rowley because I am always out in front (with Rosco I'm usually behind) and he has to try and catch me. He's still less adventurous than me and when I bound off into the undergrowth he tends to stay on the path anxiously looking for me. I try to tempt him further or "lead him astray" as David and Paulette call it. He pulls on the lead even more than me but, as Boss points out, at least he keeps *his* paws on the ground! I went back to hydrotherapy and Barbara said she was pleased with my progress although my conformation still leaves a lot to be desired. Outside we met the dog before us and the woman said, "Oh you must be the feisty young dog Barbara was telling me about." Huh! So I decided I would behave like a 10 year old instead of the 10 month old I am. I lay quietly on the vet bed, stood immaculately while I was showered and then patiently rested my head on the side of the pool while Barbara did things to my back legs. "Have you doped him?" an amazed Barbara asked. Ever heard of giving a dog a bad name...? And it was back to school too. We did a few catch-up exercises after such a long break: "stays", "downs", "waits", recalls and heel work around the other dogs. The others did their "twists" and Lesley suggested that perhaps I could learn to march but Boss has decided that she'd rather I keep all four paws firmly attached to the ground. At the end Lesley came round to say hello to each dog in turn and we were absolutely forbidden to jump up at her. I was very good and resisted the temptation to take my usual flying leap at her hair. Finally, today we went back to the vet for rabies vaccinations unintentionally leaving a lovely trail of muddy paw prints across the surgery floor after our walk by the river. They must love us! Rosco has developed a lump on the back of his neck so Jenny took a needle sample but unlike *my* fancy lump, his is just a common bit of fat and can be left alone! I thought Boss might forget about making me do heelwork every day but no such luck. Her plan of boring me is obviously working as I am getting better. Of course when are back on the shoot tomorrow with all the excitement of the other dogs, people and birds I shall probably forget everything she has been painstakingly trying to teach me – and yank her over in the mud.

Flatcoat heaven

"How lovely – a brace of flatcoats!" exclaimed one of the guns as Rosco and I headed out to the first drive. Boss explained that I was just a pup and he laughed and said "Doesn't that describe all flatcoats – they never grow up!" A pheasant fell just 15 feet me so, forgetting I was tied to a tree, I rushed to get it at the same time as Rosco. We somersaulted over each other and by the time Rosco had disentangled his legs from mine the bird had done a runner. Away went Rosco through the trees – returning with it just minutes later.

As we walked out to the drives I was very good and didn't pull but on the way back it wasn't very fair as Rosco was free to hunt for wounded or dead birds and so I did pull then because I wanted to help. Boss was going to let me stay out for the last drive but the heavens opened so she put me back in the pick-up. I don't really mind being dumped because in between drives all the others – Rosco, Rusty, Inca, Jagger and Robbie – jump in and keep me company.

Dog of the week?

Something tells me I am not going to win the Best Pup prize this week – or even the Most Popular. On an almost deserted beach Boss walked me past the only other people there with a dog and then let me off the lead when we were well past them. But I raced back to say hello and took rather a long time, I have to admit, to return to her. For that I got put back on the lead and then I pulled as hard as I could, completely forgetting all the good progress I have made in walking nicely. That night Boss had just gone to sleep when I let myself into the utility room; she heard the door open so she had to get up and let me out because she was worried that if she left me in there for too long I'd work out how to get in the food bin – something I haven't yet mastered. Yesterday we met up with Rowley and for the first time, Rosco came too as he wouldn't have had a walk otherwise. Rosco was not impressed with Rowley and kept growling at him because he wouldn't leave him alone. Like me, Rowley's not very good at getting the message when dogs don't like him! On the way back Boss borrowed Rowley's new, very expensive anti-pull collar and lead and tried it on me. I hated it and after a few minutes managed to get it off. So Boss decided there wasn't much point in her buying one (she should be grateful that for once I've actually saved her money!) but it's given her the idea of twisting my slip lead into a figure of eight which is so horrible it made me really well behaved. Of course it might be different on a shoot day... Today we went to school and did all the usual "stays" and "waits" and recall as well as weaving in and out of other dogs and meeting and greeting without jumping on them. Then Boss asked Lesley's advice about stopping me leaping up at people (I never do it to Boss). Lesley said that in eight years of running classes she'd only ever had one leaper – a GSD – and Boss said that in all the dogs she has owned she has *never* had one - until I came along. Lesley threw bits of cheese on the floor every time I sat nicely and when I leapt up she pulled me down on the ground. She explained to the others that she wouldn't do this to a nervous dog – only a bold Beau! But Boss queries as to how she can do that when she is not near enough to pull me down because when I meet people on the lead I sit perfectly quietly and they comment on how calm and well behaved I am! You see I'm not completely bonkers: I know *exactly* when I can get away with being a tearaway and when to charm people by being well behaved.

My boss – the psychopath!

Boss used the beastly figure of eight lead on me at the shoot but although I hate it I have to admit it does stop me pulling. She promises that once I grasp the idea of walking quietly at heel like Rosco, she will stop using it – it's up to me. She was so pleased that I didn't pull her over in the mud that she let me go out on all the drives before lunch. On one of them I got the closest yet to picking up a bird. Rosco was away on a long retrieve when a pheasant fell just behind us in the brambles. Worried that it might scarper, Boss and I (I was on the lead at the time rather than tied to a tree) went to get it together. I put my head right in the brambles and actually touched it but before I could grab it, Boss reached in and got it herself. She is determined to take it really slowly with me and that means no live birds at all until next season, at the very earliest. This morning we went out on the Common for a little training when suddenly we spotted the local Loopy Lulu with her two dogs. They are very friendly and if they had been off the lead, the three of us would have had a great game. Then Boss revealed that she hoped I would be a gun dog one day and Loopy Lulu hit the roof. "I can't talk to you – you're a psychopath!" she screamed as she stormed off. She yelled "psychopath, psychopath" all the way down the path! Boss was doubled up with laughter but she half admires her strong stance on all kinds of things – despite managing to get up the nose of practically everyone in the village – as she believes that everyone has a right to their own opinion. How boring it would be if we were all the same! In fact, quite a few of her friends disagree with shooting but Boss points out that as long as people shoot, picker uppers like

Rosco (and me, in the future) do a vital job of retrieving wounded birds that would otherwise die slowly in pain.

Count your blessings Boss!

Boss has been watching a television programme about borstal and it seems to be giving her funny ideas. She keeps threatening to send me to one if I don't toe the line. I have to confess I have been a bit wild this week – racing after and playing with other dogs on walks, leaping up at strangers, and getting lost in the forest. Boss doesn't mind me going on explorations but wishes I had a better sense of direction so she didn't have to stand there whistling and wondering where on earth I am. But on the up side I behaved perfectly at hydrotherapy – so much so that Barbara's assistant thought I was an *adult*! (Barbara says my topline and head position are much better ... I don't think Boss knows what that means either). And I did well at class this morning: I walked nicely to heel, stayed, waited at the gate and largely ignored all the other dogs. I think Boss should count her blessings and realise all the things I *don't* do. I don't sneak upstairs (probably because being an old cottage we have very steep, twisting and rather scary stairs). I don't chew or destroy anything. I don't steal food. I don't scrounge – even when plates of food are temptingly head height on the floor. I don't climb on the table – well, all right, only occasionally, just to have a look. I don't pull on the lead any more, even outside the classroom. I don't bite. I don't jump up at Boss. I don't bark. And I don't wake Boss up in the morning even when she sleeps in late. At not quite 11 months old, I may not be a paragon but tell me: am I really a candidate for dog borstal? Besides, where else would Boss find another furry hot water bottle for her lap on cold winter evenings?

Getting there...

"How lovely to see a working flatcoat!" exclaimed one of Saturday's guns as Rosco raced past him bearing a pheasant. It turned out he used to have one of the liver variety. He and Boss agreed that people either recognise us for what we are because they have owned or known a flatcoat, or ask if we are setters or, even more, rudely what we are crossed with. Now that I don't yank Boss into the mud I'm allowed out on nearly all the drives. She says that one of the best things about this is when we get home I don't bounce around like a lunatic; instead the three of us get on the sofa, Rosco and me flaked out and Boss behind the newspaper. Sunday was a day of rest with a leisurely stroll in the sunshine across the Common and then we were back at work again on Monday; just Barry and Boss and us four dogs. It was a memorable day because I finally managed to get a bird in my mouth – despite Boss's best intentions. Rosco was away on another retrieve when a partridge fell behind us. I dragged Boss over to it and just managed to grab it before her. Rosco receives a lot of compliments (he is a real speedy Gonzales with eyes like a hawk) but he'd better watch out: serious competition is on the way! Mind you, when he was my age he'd already been earning his keep for four months. Talk about puppy labour! One of the guns had a Labrador the same age as me and she wasn't allowed to pick anything either.

She walked perfectly at heel *off lead* but she spent the whole time whining. This is an absolute no-no. At least I keep my mouth shut.

Playdate

We should have met up with Rowley last week but he had an attack of the tummy runs. He's better now so today Boss dropped me off at his house while she took Rosco for a walk on the river bank which is just behind their house. As always, we had a terrific time charging round the garden and playing hide and seek in the conifers. Rowley is not always very bright and he chased me round and round the summer house but then suddenly his brain clicked into gear and he turned round and met me head on! When Boss came back for coffee and cake we continued playing in the kitchen. Luckily it's quite big as two large unruly pups take up a lot of room! Rowley's boss Paulette is very protective of *me* and tells him off for chewing me. What she doesn't realise — because I'm usually underneath and hidden from view — is that I am giving as good as I get! Rowley loves sucking my ears (perhaps because his are trimmed while mine are long and woolly?) while I pull his lips to make them even sloppier.

Two "firsts" for me

What a long way I have come as a potential gun dog in just four months. At the start of the season I was allowed out on only one drive and spent most of the day in the pick-up, first in the cabin and then in the back. Gradually I was allowed out on more drives but tied to something immoveable like a tree. Yesterday we went out on what is called cocks' day when it is the turn of the beaters and picker uppers to shoot as a thank you for their hard work during the season and only cock birds are shot. (Boss no longer shoots so she was just picking up). Now that I have learned to accept Rosco rushing off after pheasants without trying to join him, I didn't have to wear the harness so that I could be tied up. Instead I sat quietly with the end of the lead dropped over Boss's stick. As it was the very last day of the season Boss let me pick up my first bird: a dead partridge. While the others ate their lunch, she took me to a quiet place in the woods and threw it down for me. I played with it for a moment because, to be honest, I wasn't quite sure what I was supposed to do with it but then I picked it up and proudly carried it back to the vehicles where Boss took it from me. Boss says she can't fault me for enthusiasm and a good nose although the retrieving bit isn't quite there yet! The other "first" for me was ... snow! As we stood waiting on the last drive these fat white blobs started falling out of the sky, turning me and Rosco into Dalmatians!

Breakfast in France

I thought something was up this morning. Boss got up in what felt like the middle of the night, opened the back door to let us out and then went straight back up stairs. *No* breakfast! Did this mean yet another trip to the vet for an operation? But she was soon down again, loading stuff and us into the car and then off we went in the dark. We drove quite a long way and then on to a train. Jiggedy jig, jigged jig— it made the car rock gently. When we came off, Boss announced "You're in France boys!" Just a short while later we stopped for a run around and breakfast on the roadside. *Not* what we are used to! Then we drove on and on and on, stopping to stretch our legs every three hours or so. Rosco and I were very good, quietly watching France go by out of the window but if this is Boss's idea of a holiday ... well, frankly, I'd rather stay at home. After 16 hours on the road, we finally stopped at what I was told was a hotel. I jumped on the bed and was promptly told to get off; Rosco gave me one of his headmaster looks: "Can't you at least try to behave!" But I've never seen a bed before so how was I to know it wasn't a big sofa? I was allowed though to inspect the bathroom which I thought was fascinating. I tried to eat the soap but it didn't taste very nice and it wasn't very easy to drink the water out of the loo. Meanwhile Boss lay on the big bed with a glass of wine and the paper and Rosco curled up on his bed on the floor and went to sleep. I suppose they're used to all this or perhaps they know something I don't...

Supper in Spain

Another early start and back in the car. Just minutes later Boss said, "*Au revoir* France and *hola Espana*!" And then the snow started and Boss thought it was too deep and cold to stop so decided to press on. Finally we drove into an underground garage and Boss told us we could play in the garden while she unpacked the car. Wow! The snow was several inches deep and this was the real stuff, not like those wet Suffolk blobs. Rosco and I had huge fun tearing round and round and rolling in it. Then I discovered that I could squeeze myself through the gate and after a moment's hesitation, Rosco happily followed suit. Away we went down the snowy street to explore the village. I am not exaggerating when I say Boss was *incandescent* with rage – ie she was all lit up, she was so angry. Tails between our legs we snuck back into the garden but then I refused to come indoors as Boss got crosser and crosser. It was such heaven playing in the snow after being stuck in the car for so long ... but finally she tricked me into going in. It then took me a long time to go up the stairs because I've never been up stairs before. But once in the apartment I stuck my nose into every room and cupboard. Now I'm going to curl up in front of the woodburner while outside a blizzard is raging and the high pitched howl of the wind is so wolf-like that every now and then Rosco and I sit up and listen, a little worried that a pack is going to burst in the door. But Boss seems oblivious and it is very cosy in here so we settle back down. I think I'm going to like Spain – even though Boss says I am not allowed in the garden unsupervised because of my great escape (apparently in 10 years neither Titus nor Rosco ever got out – how unadventurous of them is all I can say!) But is this a holiday or are we going to live here forever? Not that it matters because "home" is wherever Boss is.

Meet and greet

Boss has a funny little Spanish car where we sit just behind her on the back seat rather than stuck behind a grid in the very back of the Volvo. This means we have to wear harnesses so that we don't go flying through the windscreen. Having to get dressed up is a bit of a bore but at least we get to drive to lovely walks. Since we arrived, we have met various people: Boss's friend Sonia and her son Victor who played with Rosco (I was in the doghouse that day because I'd pulled the telephone on to the floor, broken an alarm clock and some ceramic things Boss had made, and eaten a pen while she was out for lunch and I was bored); Mariano who came to fix a leak in the kitchen; two men who carried in the gas; one of the neighbours who made a big fuss of me and said he didn't mind at all when I jumped up to lick his face; Alicia who cleans the stairs, and Juan who brought logs for the fire. Boss reminds me that curiosity killed the cat (or flatcoat) as I am into everything. I love looking in all the drawers and cupboards, the washing machine, the bath, the woodburner (no, not when it's alive, stupid), wherever I can possibly poke my nose. In the mornings it is such a novelty to find Boss in bed that I like to reassure her that I am there. I go round both sides of the bed and sniff and put a paw up but there is no response although I am sure she is just pretending to be asleep. So then I poke my nose under the bottom of the duvet and lick her toes. That does the trick! Though I have to admit she lets out such an indignant roar when it is 2am that I skate back to my own bed as quickly as I can on the skiddy tiled floor. I haven't yet learned the wisdom of letting sleeping bosses lie... I hear an awful lot of "Beau get off," "Beau get out," "Beau go away". But I don't take any notice. Today I'm not the world's most popular dog for pulling Boss over so that she dropped her keys in the snow and it's so deep she won't find them until it thaws! Huh – her fault for putting me on the lead in the *garden!* I do *try* to be good but life is just so exciting... the problem with Boss and Rosco is typical old age: disapproval of and irritation with the young and a desire to spend far too much time asleep when they could be out *living!*

Pup's law

Today we climbed a mountain that seemed very high to me; after all, I am a boy of flat Suffolk. I saw huge birds gliding silently just above us and I watched in amazement as I'd never realised birds could have such massive wings. There were so many new and different smells and I ran all over the place. The only problem with going off piste is that I get lost as I seem to have no sense of direction. It is pup's law that every single time I emerge back on the path I turn the wrong way. For once, it's a relief to hear Boss's pesky whistle. Boss keeps wittering on about the dangers of disappearing off into the undergrowth and meeting wild boar. (We have a stuffed boar's head at home – called Alfonso - and I have to admit those great big teeth look a little scary but I'm confident that if I met one he'd be sure to like me and want to play, rather than kill me as per Boss's dire warnings). There are also wolves here in the mountains; apparently some killed 30 goats just a few weeks ago. But surely they can tell the difference between a tender goat and a tough flatcoat? We met a group of mountain bikers who said *"Hola!"* To give them a taste of English friendliness I jumped up and ... they promptly fell off! It was a long walk so Boss sat down a couple of times (she said it was to admire the view but I think to catch her breath) and offered us biscuits. But I didn't have time to stop and eat – I was far too busy exploring, up and down, everywhere. Tired? I don't even know what that means ... until we get home when I am out like a light.

A partridge, a rude runner and a Spanish dog

On our walk today I found a dead partridge. I was *so* pleased with myself! Rosco tried to take it off me but no chance – finders' keepers. Eventually I gave it to Boss. We walked up and down lots of little paths and at one point I got lost having turned the wrong way as usual. I could hear the whistle but couldn't work out where it was coming from. When I finally spotted Boss's waving arms it was a very tough climb back to her. We walked a long way but at one point we sat down for a picnic in the sunshine: bread and ham for Boss and biscuits for me and Rosco. We came upon two men with mountain motorbikes. They were very friendly which is more than can be said for the lone runner we met a bit later. I jumped around him and he raised his arms which I assumed was an invitation to jump even higher. I didn't understand what he was shouting – something about *Dios*? – but I don't think it was very polite. Then I met my first Spanish dog: a pretty golden retriever who was a little shy but friendly. Although there is still deep dazzling snow – no sign of the keys yet – there wasn't a cloud in the sky. And it was hot enough for us to sit on the *terrazza* when we got home.

You can't catch me – I'm Top Dog!

Boss says I am getting far too cocky and full of myself. Once upon a time I returned and stopped on the whistle; now I just turn a deaf ear. I don't want to get in the car at the end of a walk even when

I'm exhausted, go indoors when I'm busy playing in the snow in the garden, or go on the lead. In fact, I don't want to do as I'm told, full stop. I suspect there are times when Boss is so exasperated with me that she is tempted to feed me to the wolves and wild boar. I'm just as badly behaved to Rosco. When we're out walking Rosco likes to carry something like a stick or a fir cone but whatever he's got, *I* want. After a while, Rosco gives up and lets me have it. I carry it for a bit and then lose interest and drop it. Patient Rosco picks it up so of course I want it back – and the game starts all over again. If I can't pull it off him then I grab him tightly round the back legs and hump him for all I'm worth knowing that will make him swing round to throw me off and let go of whatever it is in the attempt. Boss says I am a bully and a spoilt brat and urges Rosco to take me down a peg or three. But he is far too placid a chap to retaliate. So this after-noon Boss decided to try and punish me herself. Rosco is obsessed with his balls (why are you sniggering?) and his favourite game is to chase after one, bring it back and then chase after a second that Boss throws in another direction. He will chase after them until he – or Boss - collapses in a heap. But because I keep grabbing his tail and humping him, she thinks I am spoiling his fun. So she made me stay in the hallway where I could see them playing through the glass doors. Will it teach me a lesson? I doubt it!

Mad but madly happy

We had just a shortish walk this morning in the falling snow beside the river which was racing along between steep cliffs. I tried to get a closer look but Boss was worried I would overbalance: even Rosco wouldn't manage to swim in those rapids let alone me with funny back legs. Then she left us – in the hall so that I didn't get up to mischief – for what felt like hours. She's left us home alone here before: to have lunch with Sonia or go to the shop. We're not allowed to go in the village as there are lots of dogs hanging out in the street and if they saw a new kid on the block – well, fur would fly! Today, it seems she drove to Madrid and went to an art gallery. She said she thought of me when she read this quotation of Goya in a letter to Martin Zapater in 1785: "The dog has done many good things, although he was a bit sloppy at fetching; he squeezed the first partridge too tight, and did not want to bring it; then, after a lot of coaxing, he started to retrieve the rabbits (...) but I am madly happy with him." Though I drive her mad at times, I know Boss too is madly happy with me – well, I think she is...

A skull and leg bone!

High on the mountain I found the skull of a cow, complete with all its teeth. I carried it for a bit but it was very heavy. And then I found a great big leg bone. I knew cows were big but I didn't realise how big because you don't often find bits of cow in Suffolk... I find other things too like gloves, hats, water bottles, once a condom and best of all, a very smart pair of striped man's pants. I can understand why someone might want to take their knickers off on a mountain but why would they forget to put them back on?

Head in the clouds

We set off up the mountain hardly able to see a foot in front of us because we were in dense cloud. But when we got to the top we burst out into sunshine, looking down on swirls of cloud. It was like walking in the air! Anti-social Boss loves the way we can walk for hours and never see anyone; personally I'd rather meet lots of people. But on the way down my luck was in because we met a group of cyclists. Why anyone in their right mind would want to bike or run up a mountain is beyond me; they miss out on all those delicious sniffs, to say nothing of yummy old bones. One of them said *Que bonito!* (how handsome). I'm sure he was looking at me but Rosco was convinced it was him. And whilst on the subject of looks, I have gone off Boss's friend Sonia in a big way. She looked at us both and said she thought Rosco was the most handsome. I couldn't believe my ears. Is she stupid – or in need of glasses? How could anyone think that that greybeard is better looking than me?

Settling down

We have been in Spain for two weeks now and as I get used to the change of life I am much better behaved. For example, I am remembering what the whistle is for and I no longer make a fuss about getting in the car at the end of a walk or coming indoors from the garden. Boss hates doing the same thing every day but we dogs love routine because it helps us know where we are and what is what. Our day starts at 8am when I tell Boss it's time to get up. I find jumping on the bed and sitting on her is the most effective method.

Then she makes a coffee, has a shower (I play peekaboo round the curtain), gets dressed and takes us in the garden for p&p and 10 minutes of crazy racing games. Back in then for breakfast while she washes up and cleans out the fire. We have to sit just outside the front door while she sweeps and mops the floor and then it's into the little car that Boss calls Esperanza (because it means hope and driving such an ancient car round Spain, we probably need it) and off we go for a walk somewhere. In the fortnight we have been here we haven't walked the same walk twice – despite walking every single day. Sometimes she takes a picnic, other times she stops off for a meal on the way back while we sit patiently in the car waiting for ours. Then it's home, supper and fast asleep in front of the fire. Some days Boss goes out during the day or the evening but basically our days are pretty much the same. Last thing at night, Boss takes us out in the garden with me on a lead as it is so dark she cannot see if there is a cat (they are regular visitors and one has only three legs so it certainly couldn't out-run or out-climb two flatcoats). She also wouldn't be able to see if I escaped. Finally, Rosco and I curl up on our beds in front of the dying fire, dreaming of everything we have seen and smelt.

Wild dogs

I have learned that wolves, wild boar, foxes and deer all roam the mountains but today I discovered there are also wild dogs! We were walking where there are no paths, just wandering at will through ancient oaks and scrubby bushes far from any *fincas* or villages.

114

Suddenly we came upon a big, fierce-looking, reddish brown dog. He stood looking at us for a moment as shocked by our encounter as we were; then Boss yelled, grabbed the two of us, hurriedly hauling us away and the dog fled. (When Boss yells it's enough to make anyone run for the hills). I wanted to follow him and say *Hola* but Boss was adamant: absolutely not. It seems that some of the dogs that hang out in the village make their way into the mountains where they live off whatever they can find: young deer or collapsed old cows. I like my creature comforts - like regular meals I don't have to hunt for and a warm, cosy bed – so I don't think it's a life that would appeal to me.

Poo!

After 10 months together I've learned that my boss has some un-usual interests (aeroplanes, shooting, fishing, churches and long lonely walks to name but a few) but now she has a new one: poo! Today on our walk, she kept poking poo with her stick trying to de-termine who or what had left it. It turns out that yesterday she went to an exhibition on poo in Madrid (and I thought she was being cul-tural, going to art galleries!) and now she is trying to work out what is in the vicinity: wild boar, deer, wolves or goats. Whilst on the sub-ject of what comes out, Rosco and I are now putting Spanish food in at the other end. No, not paella (although we did have some fresh anchovies the other day when she'd cooked too many) but a chicken and rice kibble that is not really very different from our usual English fare.

Honey trap

When Boss said we were going to climb a mountain called the Honey Peak I thought oh yummy. But what a con! There was no honey at all – not even any beehives (and there are usually lots of those because the bees feed on all the mountain thyme and rosemary). But it was a great walk up and then down steep narrow paths in total silence. I find the quiet in the mountains very odd; I keep looking and listening to see why I can't hear anything or anybody (is there something blocking my ears?): no aeroplanes, cars, people, dogs, nothing. And above the tree line there isn't even any bird song. Just those gigantic silent birds, circling above us without even flapping their wings that Boss says are vultures.

Just like the Queen

If the Queen can have two birthdays, so can I! Today is my official birthday in that I was born a year ago. But I have decided that my real life started when I met Boss so that is the date I am going to celebrate as my birthday proper. Before then, I was just one of 10 puppies and lots of other adult dogs but here I am somebody very special. As a treat we had pasta, rice and chicken mixed in with our kibble. Actually, I think the idea was to fatten up Rosco who lost a lot of weight during the shooting season. Unlike me who would happily scoff as much as Boss chooses to give me, Rosco is not interested in food and some days opts to eat nothing at all.

The rain in Spain ....

...simply doesn't fall! After three weeks here, I have just seen the first rain which was only a little drizzle as it was getting dark. We have had snow, ice, wind and sunshine but no rain at all up until now. Today I saw hares for the first time – too fast for me and even for Rosco – and great big black and white birds with long beaks and even longer spindly pink legs sitting on very untidy nests on top of masts and pylons and the church tower. Boss says they are storks, who have flown in from Africa.

Legless

Not the best start to today: Rosco was coughing and throwing up and one of my front legs was quite painful so I was hobbling. So Boss took us for just a short run by the river before leaving us to go to Madrid. So much for sympathy! By the time she returned, Rosco was fine but my leg is still sore. To be honest, it's not so bad that I can't try and race around the garden with Rosco but I hope it's better for tomorrow or we may have to miss out on our usual lovely long walks. Boss says she saw today a 19th century painting of a French aristocrat and his family and what was definitely a flatcoat at their feet. She said he looked just like me. On the days Boss goes to Madrid, she usually plays with us in the garden when she gets home to make up for hours of abandonment but not today because ... it's snowing again.

Rosco the poser

My leg is 100% again; Boss thinks perhaps I twisted it on the very slippery ceramic floors we have here. So we went for a lovely long walk in the wind and sunshine. Boss likes to take pictures of us posing in front of views of the mountains. Rosco is such a poser that he happily leaps up to wherever she wants him but I'm far too busy to ponce around for pictures and I don't fancy climbing on to some of the rocks she tries to persuade me on to. I am nothing like as surefooted as Rosco; there are stairs up to the apartment which obviously I manage but I take them slowly and carefully, whereas Rosco hares up and down them without a second thought. But as proof that wisdom comes with age and experience: I now pay much more attention to where Boss is on our walks as I have realised that in this vast, wild, empty landscape I could easily get lost.

Perdon! Lo siento!

Just as we were going back to the car park today I spied two people. Whooppee! I raced over to say _Hola,_ totally ignoring Boss's whistle and yelling. I jumped all around them until Boss rushed up, apologising profusely for my behaviour. The two men were very nice and said they realised I was young. Boss said that is not an excuse. She told me to sit and I did, instantly. The men were impressed and said, "_muy bien_." As Boss put my lead on, she said no, he is not good, he is _muy mal_ (which I think probably means "awful.") She hauled me away which was a shame because two more men appeared that I could have said *Hola* to. Boss was not amused: "I do not want to spend the rest of my life apologising for you."

Say what you mean, mean what you say

The forecast for today was good so Boss said we would have to get up early to walk before the crowds came. Every weekend they pour into the village in their hundreds, laden with skis and toboggans, to escape the hustle and bustle of Madrid. (Rosco and I don't need a sled: we simply roll in the snow and slide down the slopes on our backs!) So I jumped on her bed at 3am – well, she did say early.... You should have heard the roar as she kicked me off. But by 9am we were on the mountain and just two hours later, back in the sun on the *terrazza*. I love sitting here because there is so much to look at: storks flying down to the water for a drink, people walking with and without dogs by the lake, cyclists and sometimes, the yellow helicopter taking the dead and wounded off the mountains. Of course in England, we'd be in our garden but this one is shared so we can't mooch about as we would normally. I only found out that other people live here yesterday when suddenly we heard noises. Rosco barked and I hurriedly checked out the bedrooms, the bath-room and the kitchen but there was nobody there. Spooky! I finally worked out that there was someone outside our apartment and I sat at the front door hopefully wagging my tail. But then it all went quiet again. I hadn't realised other people lived here: the front door and staircase lead to just four apartments but the other three are all empty and apparently another 11 people live in the other apartments. It has been so hot today that I am glad our walk was early so that we can now just lie and pant on the cool floor. And it's only March 1st!

Superfit Superdog!

Today was our longest walk yet: four and a half hours! (We nearly didn't make the walk at all as Boss got Esperanza stuck before we'd even started!). The snow was really deep in places so Boss had to take it quite slowly. I suppose that's the problem with only having two legs. At the very top we sat in the sunshine looking down on the village and the lake, the three of us sharing an empanada. When we got home, I had a quick sleep but now I'm full of beans ready to make mischief. "Why aren't you tired?" moaned Boss. But I'm not sore or stiff or tired at all so I must be a superfit Superdog.

These things just happen

It was a really snowy walk this morning. Boss was up to her knees at times and I disappeared into a deep drift on one occasion. I tried to climb a pine tree – much to Boss's amusement – because there were a couple of red squirrels making faces at me from the branches, but they were much too agile for me. I am determined though to catch one of the many lizards that dash around our front steps. They are super quick as they disappear into cracks in the concrete; a bit like the mice and their holes in the garden in England. In the afternoon Boss left us to go into Madrid, for once trusting us with the run of the apartment (well, I say "us" but of course I mean me as Rosco never does anything he shouldn't). We slept for a while and then I was bored so had fun pulling to pieces a rush brush that Boss uses to clean out the fire and then I chewed one of the logs. For some reason the phone ended up upside down on the floor – I can't think how – but it still works. Sometimes these things just happen and at least I didn't do anything really awful.

Dice with death

Boss warned me of the dangers of wild boar and wolves in the mountains but not the Spanish driver with murder on his mind. We were walking on one of the mountain tracks – as it happens, a recognised hiking/biking trail – when suddenly a 4 by 4 came screaming round the corner. I ran towards him and as soon as he saw me he accelerated and, rather than swerving to avoid me, drove straight at me. He missed me by a hair. He and Boss shouted at each other in Spanish for some time; finally he drove off and we walked on. But Boss was shaken at how close she had come to going home with just one dog. I don't know how many lives dogs have but she reckons I certainly used up one of them today.

Phew!

The last few days have been getting hotter and hotter but today was the hottest to date. Wall to wall deep blue sky and not a cloud in sight. So what does Boss do? Takes us up the one and only mountain where there is not a drop to drink! Usually there are lots of streams from the melting snow. So at the summit we drank *her* bottle of water out of the cover of her rucksack. We saw nobody else – not even a mad Spanish driver! - the whole walk. What is it that they say about mad Englishwomen and their dogs in the mid-day sun? It was too hot to leave us in the car so we all came home for a late lunch. The apartment was very cool and it was good to stretch out on those ceramic floors. *Now* I understand why the Spanish don't have carpets like the English do.

Happy birthday Rosco!

Today Rosco is eight years old – or perhaps I should say young because when we are racing around together people always ask "*Which* is the young one?" I know he didn't think much of me at the beginning but now we are the very best of buddies. We do absolutely everything together: drink, eat, sleep, pee, poo and play. If, on a walk, one of us is missing the other always waits – even though Boss stalks off, ignoring us both. I know there are times when I am bored and he must get fed up with me – like when I bite his legs so he has to do a sort of St Vitus dance to avoid my snapping jaws. But he has never really told me off. "More's the pity" says Boss. One thing he loves that I do – and something which Boss certainly doesn't do - is when I poke my long pink tongue into his ears: he puts his head on one side, closes his eyes and smiles. It seems to be getting hotter and hotter and today Boss cut short our walk because of the heat as even I was beginning to slow down. When we got back to the car I drank and drank and then threw up all over the grass. Boss was just pleased it wasn't in Esperanza. Once home, I drank even more and then crashed out in the cool before, some hours later, Boss gave us our special birthday meal: chicken, rice and pasta. Apparently we have to get into double figures before we get a yummy birthday cake made with chicken, liver, carrots and apples and "iced" with cream cheese and yogurt. Rosco has only two more years to go but I have a very long wait!

PEOPLE!

As you may have gathered, I have been seriously deprived of human company (I don't count Boss) whilst we have been here. But not to-day! We walked really early before it got too hot for just under three hours and then when we were nearly back at the car I spotted a man. He was quite a way off but I didn't mind: I raced over to say *Hola* and he waved his stick at me and caught me with it a few times. Then just as Boss was about to put me on the lead I spotted something way below us through the trees. Finally I trudged back up to where Boss was waiting and then before she could grab me I spotted PEOPLE – lots of them – out of the corner of my eye! I couldn't believe my luck; I charged over to them and leaped around them all. I was having so much fun that I completely ignored Boss and darted away when she tried to catch me. A mortified Rosco sat down pretending I was nothing to do with him. Eventually I gave in and let Boss haul me away to the car. Think I am probably the most unpopular dog in the world just now – and keeping a low profile might be a smart move. Anyway, on the subject of embarrassment, can there be anything worse than Boss who, to avoid sunburn, insists on walking with a face covered in white stuff? She bears a remarkable resemblance to a clown...

In at the deep end

Boss decided that immersion in icy cold water might protect us from the possibility of heatstroke so today we walked round a huge lake. You might think this would be an easy walk on the level but you don't know Boss and you don't know Spain! The banks were very steep and rocky so we had to keep clambering up and over and round. The water was shallow for about two feet and then it suddenly dropped hundreds of feet. I was happy to paddle in the shallows but Rosco loved plunging out into the deep water after sticks and stones. Then we had a long dusty climb back up to the car by which time we were hot, dry and very, very thirsty again despite having tried to drink the lake dry. No people to jump on, no crazy Spanish drivers, no cows, no dogs, *nada b*ut we three...

Not one of the best

Funny old weekend... Yesterday we got in the Volvo rather than Esperanza – what a surprise! And then we drove for what seemed like hours into a city. Lots to look at and then we drove out through deserted hills where Boss stopped to let us stretch our legs. It was very unfair because I had to stay on a lead while Rosco was free to explore (this could be because when we stopped to fill up with diesel I nearly pulled Boss over in my enthusiasm to get to two rabbits sitting cheekily watching us). Then, lots more stops and each time we got excited at the thought of getting out but no, Boss was simply taking pictures. At one point Boss stopped to eat her sandwich but since she had forgotten to take anything for us, she shared her bread and ham with us, as well as tortilla. Eventually we stopped for quite a while because Boss was looking round the birthplace of some bloke called Goya. The guide woman had spotted us sitting patiently in the car and asked to meet us: the highlight of our day. She thought we were beautiful and made a big fuss of us but had never heard of our breed. (Actually lots of people in the UK, never mind Spain, have never heard of flatcoated retrievers). I gave her a big English kiss which she loved! It was very late and dark by the time we arrived home but Boss said because we had been such good boys we could have "extras" of sardines and broccoli with our supper. Then today, Sunday, we were up early for a brilliant walk – as compensation for no walk yesterday – up the mountain behind the village. After picking up papers, bread and empanada (it comes hot from the oven and smells fabulous), Boss abandoned us to go into Madrid. It has gone very cold and snowy again here but whatever the weather we have been promised that tomorrow is all ours: no endless hours in the car and no abandonment.

Dead deer – or bits of...

Boss kept her promise today: we walked for nearly five hours, including biscuit breaks and playing in the river. She hadn't intended to walk so far but thanks to the snow, we missed her usual path. We walked up a mountain and then down another side and back beside the river. There wasn't a cloud in the sky but it was not as hot as it has been and besides, we were mostly walking in the shade of the pines, there were lots of little streams for drinking out of and paddling in, and snow to roll in. We didn't see any live deer – let alone humans – but I found two bits of dead ones. First, a head with all its teeth and hair (but no eyes) which Boss was happy for me to carry it until I tried to eat it. She took it off me, made me and Rosco stay and then threw it over a rock into the rapids of the river, I think. I searched and searched for it and when Boss walked on and whistled I joined her but then when she thought I had forgotten about it I raced back for another look. Finally, because I didn't want to be left behind and Boss clearly had no intention of waiting for me, I gave up. Then I found the leg of a deer. Again Boss took it off me and this time, slung it over the branch of a tree. I jumped, I leaped, I wrapped my front legs round the trunk, I did my utmost to grab it – without success. Again Boss walked on and again I had to go back to keep trying. Finally I gave up and we went home, had lunch and I fell asleep for an hour. If I had done this sort of walk when we first arrived, I suppose I would have been shattered. But now I am as fit as a fiddle and Boss is stunned - and probably disappointed - that I am not out for the count. Perhaps this is the remedy for deformed legs: run up and down mountains every day? As the sun went down, wonders will never cease, Boss washed the Volvo. I've never seen her do that before but I gather it's because it was covered in salt after the drive here in snow and ice. While she was busy sloshing water around, Rosco sunbathed and I tried to catch those lizards....

I readily admit that...

...sometimes I am deliberately naughty like when I jump all over people despite Boss yelling and whistling. Or when I spoil Rosco's fun by grabbing hold of his tail or humping him. Then, Boss grabs me, gives me a little shake, eyeballs me and says crossly, "You are *not* –absolutely *not* - to do that." I look suitably submissive and sorry but then, when she releases me, I go back to doing exactly what I was doing before! But other times it is accidental like when I was playing with Rosco, biting and pulling at his neck and broke his Scalibor collar. (All the time we have been here we have been wearing these funny white collars – in addition to the usual ones – as protection against diseases like leishmaniasis. This is not a time of the year we are likely to get it but super neurotic Boss refuses to take any chances). So we went to a big animal foodstuffs shop to buy another. Guarding the place at the back was a massive mastiff who wagged his tail when he saw Boss but then he spotted us in the car and went ballistic. Rosco was leaping up and down, barking back, but I just sat very quietly in the corner of the seat, making myself as small as possible. I was very glad that he was behind a very big fence and we were safe in the car.

Where vultures dare

After a quick stop by the river for p&p we headed north for what seemed like forever. Eventually we came to a reserve for birds of prey and we walked by the river in a steep gorge. There were towering cliffs on either side which had lots of holes and we saw loads of those huge birds that I now know are vultures going in and out of them and sitting on the top watching us. These great big birds with their outstretched wings and white heads fascinate me: I could watch them for ages. In fact it's probably the only time I stand still. It was a terrific walk but the less we say of the man I jumped on after I'd been in the river, the better... The rest of the day was a bit boring as Boss simply drove and got in and out to buy cases of wine and take pictures of monasteries and castles. Esperanza may be much smaller than the Volvo but you'd be surprised how well Rosco and I squash together on the back seat. And because we had had a nice walk with the vultures we didn't complain or fidget at all.

Pigs of both kinds

Somebody left the garden gate open and I escaped into the road and found ... a pet pig! Wow! Was this exciting! It was going for a walk with its owner and although I was desperate to make friends with it, it didn't seem very keen to reciprocate. Finally, the owner caught hold of the pig and Boss grabbed me. Boss was very apologetic, explaining that the gate had been left open, but the pig's owner was very nice and told her not to worry. Then, we were playing in the garden with Boss when a neighbour and her friends came out. I jumped up and the man kicked me and Boss rushed up and he hit her so hard that she fell over on her back into the hard stones – despite the fact that *she* hadn't done anything. The man – a human pig of the worst kind – then roared off in his car. Boss says I will be the death of her. Literally.

Spanish vet

This morning we had a relatively short walk – only an hour of racing around the mountain – and then drove to Madrid where we saw Pablo, Boss's Spanish vet. He weighed us (I am the same weight as I was before we left England two months ago and Rosco has gained a kilo), looked in our ears, eyes and mouth (stupidly, he looked in Rosco's just after he had given him a treat so it promptly fell out and I gobbled it up!) and took our blood pressure. Pablo said he thought we were both very fit, healthy, good looking dogs. As he saw us out, he gave Boss a huge hug and kiss.

Fried Rosco

In the paper there was a recipe for *Roscos Fritos* (his name is Spanish for a type of ring doughnut). Normally Rosco never puts a paw wrong but today he came the closest ever to being fried. On our walk I found a deer skin (somebody else had scoffed all the innards) which Rosco snatched off me. Boss walked on and whistled for us to come. I was torn: stay with Rosco who had no intention of sharing "his" trophy or follow Boss who was out of sight by this time? I decided to run after Boss but Rosco ignored her. Mind you, as she stormed back he saw he was in *big* trouble and immediately dropped the deer skin. Boss kept us both on leads until we had gone far enough for neither of us to race back.

Something's up...

A lot more snow fell last night so instead of walking in the mountains we went to the river where there was just a sprinkling. So far so good but then Boss started packing the Volvo. The underground garage is very big as everybody in the apartments parks their cars there and I had great fun, painstakingly carrying somebody's logs up to our place and then I found a net of kindling. How was I to know there was a hole in the bottom so pieces of wood dropped out all the way up the stairs? Boss was *not* pleased. She said she'd got more than enough to do without sweeping up after me. Meanwhile Rosco sat around looking worried until Boss stopped packing and played with his balls (stop sniggering – it's *so* childish). Finally she locked up, told us to get in the car and off we went. Not very far, as it turned out: only to Boss's favourite restaurant where she had a quick lunch. From there we drove on and on and on. We stopped at a place for our meal and she said we were back in France. Then back into the car again and on for a long time until finally we stopped at a hotel for the night. I think I could grow accustomed to hotel life: we sleep on our beds right next to Boss's big bed so she is never out of our sight and it's all very cosy.

Beach heaven!

A quick breakfast and then it was back in the car again for what seemed like forever. We stopped a couple of times to stretch our legs (Rosco off the lead but not me – wild child that I am). And then we ground to a halt on the road because there in front of us was a lorry on fire with a huge column of black smoke pouring from it. It was quite hot – from the sun, not the fire – so Boss gave us water and then walked us along the road as seven fire engines roared past us. It was quite exciting at first because everyone got out of their cars and lorries to have a look at what was happening and of course, to say hello to us. But then as time wore on, it got a bit boring. Finally we were allowed to drive on and then Boss took us to the seaside. What a beach! There was a massive expanse of sand and dunes and after being cooped up in the car for so long, Rosco and I just ran and ran, chased each other in circles and rolled in the sand. Anyone would think we had just been released from a year in kennels! I met three little French dogs and I lay down on my back to show them that although I am big and black and British I am really very friendly. Unfortunately a woman was less playful because I chased all the birds off. How was I to know she was trying to take photographs? At least we assumed that she wasn't very happy from all the yelling and gesticulating because although Boss speaks Spanish she clearly hasn't a word of French. That's the advantage of being a dog: we all have the sense to speak the same lingo. I don't know why humans aren't that bright. The sun was setting as we piled back into the car and drove on. But not for very long because then we got out and went into an office where a woman checked our chips and passports. Back into the car and on to the jiggedy-jig train again. It was very dark and late when eventually we got out – back at our English cottage. This was a shock! I had completely forgotten my home back here (eyes like a hawk, nose like a bloodhound and head like a sieve). You have to understand that I have spent nearly a sixth of my short life in Spain and had assumed that that was my forever home. Boss let us run round the garden and then we got back into our old beds under the table and she went upstairs to where, I now realize, *her* bed is.

Readjusting

It was wet and windy this morning – *not* what we are accustomed to! - but at least it was nice to play and explore the garden without Boss's constant supervision. She spent a lot of time unloading the car and putting stuff away while we zoomed in and out, leaving wet muddy paw prints everywhere, finding old toys and generally getting in the way. Boss was irritated that we were so full of beans with our noses into absolutely everything – well, mine anyway – but she doesn't understand: we are used to lovely long hikes not just a garden exploration. Where are the mountains? The freedom to race around? The snow to bite and roll in? It's lucky we dogs just get on with life and readily adapt to something new and different without looking back or regretting – unlike Boss....

Is England too small and overcrowded for me?

On our first day back in the UK Boss didn't take us for a walk at all – partly because it was raining although that doesn't normally stop her but mainly I think because she is fed up and missing Spain. But yesterday she took pity on us and we went to the forest. I was quite good for most of the walk but then I went straight though a gate and on to the road. Seconds after I returned a car whizzed by at top speed. Phew! Another life gone! Then when we were nearly back at the car my eagle eye spotted a chocolate Labrador and I raced off to say hello, turning a deaf ear to Boss's whistle. Hugo was quite young too and delighted to see me – which is more than can be said for Boss when she finally caught up with me. The trouble is, I got so used to running free in Spain where there are no roads or people that being back here is proving quite a shock.

Rowley and the rabbit

Life has been pretty boring since we got back. We go for walks but they are much shorter and a lot less interesting than what we have been used to. There have been two - unconnected - highlights in the last week: my mate Rowley and a rabbit. Boss dropped me off to play with Rowley while she took Rosco for a walk. It was good to see him again after so long but he is *so* exhausting! At times I stretched out on the kitchen floor pretending to be fast asleep while he poked me with his paw urging me to get up and play. Trotting up and down Spanish mountains is far less tiring! The other thrill was catching a rabbit. The garden is supposedly rabbit-proofed to prevent them getting in and destroying Boss's flowers but now and then an entrepreneur tunnels his way in. Rosco and I were convinced that there was at least one under the garden shed and we dug and dug and – unfortunately – have made quite a mess of the shed. But it was worth it because suddenly one shot out and *I* caught it. Rosco immediately came up and said "I'll take that" and snatched it off me but not for long because Boss went up to him and said "I'll have that" and took it off *him*!

The Great Escape

Boss and her friend Gwen were yakking away in the kitchen over a cup of coffee. When those two get together, the world could stop and they wouldn't notice - so what better time to put my plan into action! I'd been thinking that if a rabbit could tunnel under the fence *into* the garden then surely two flatcoats could tunnel their way *out*? I dug and dug – with a bit but not much help from Rosco – and I had just emerged on to the Common with Rosco behind me in the tunnel when Boss and Gwen came out. Talk about bad timing! Another five minutes and we'd have been well away. Instead she grabbed us both and has now filled up the hole with bricks and rubble.

If at first you don't succeed...

...try again! Boss was busy stacking logs and I was standing at the back of the garden looking out over the field behind when I spotted some rabbits hopping into the garden next door. Irresistible! I squeezed through a hole in the fence and followed them. Rotten Rosco gave the game away by going and telling Boss I'd gone. (He nudges, pushes and prods until she gets the message). She went round into the garden (the house is empty) and found me investigating a huge warren. I saw her coming and quickly thought Oh no! She's going to take me home. So I darted round her and ran through the garden straight on to the road. I set off down it with Boss in hot pursuit and turned into a driveway to explore somebody's open garage. "Is everything OK Deborah?" called Sue, a neighbour. "No!

Can you try and grab him if he makes a bolt for it?" As Boss came round one side of the car I charged out – straight into a rugby tackle from Sue. Boss says with cars speeding along this road I am very, very lucky: Sue undoubtedly saved my life. The hole in the fence has now been netted so no more tunnelling or climbing my way to freedom. And just to make sure I don't try exiting at the front, there are now extensions on the fence there. Talk about Colditz – with Boss as the Camp Commandant!

Spot the difference!

Once a month Boss delivers the village newsletter to neighbours on the Common and this time she decided to take me with her as an exercise in lead work and patience. At the first house they wanted Boss to go in for a coffee but she refused to tie me up in the garden so they talked on the doorstep for *ages*. After a bit I gave up trying to get the biscuit crumbs they'd put out for the birds and lay down in resignation. "Isn't he calm and laid-back!" they declared. Which just goes to show how dumb some humans are: that they can't tell the difference between good behaviour and utter boredom. It didn't get any better as everybody wanted to hear about our holiday in Spain and Boss wanted to catch up on the latest local gossip. I sincerely hope that next month Boss delivers the newsletters by herself.

New school

Loads of people and about 50 dogs (spaniels, yellow and black Labradors and golden retrievers but no flatcoats): my idea of heaven! But as I bounced about and tried to say hello to them all, Boss firmly reminded me that I was there to learn not play as this was gun dog school. There were five of us in the puppy class, working outside in a very big field. We could see and hear other classes for the grown up dogs which was hugely tempting as it looked as though they were having a lot more fun than us. Julie, the trainer, made us walk to heel really, really slowly. Boss has always walked quite quickly and although I say it myself, on the whole I am very good at not pulling but we've never done this funereal stroll before. Julie says that if bosses walk fast they are walking at the dog's pace not theirs which Boss readily admitted was a good and very valid point. We were all pretty awful at this except for a very young Labrador that has clearly been to the titbit school of training as she followed her boss's hand and treat. Julie pointed out that treating retrievers can prove a problem later so it looks like she agrees with Boss on the subject which is a shame. Finally Julie threw a dummy in front of each of us and while she held the dog, the boss had to walk out and pick up the dummy. The class was quite short as, like all youngsters, we have a very limited attention span and we were beginning to fidget. Our "homework" is to do the slow walk to heel three times a day. Ugh!

Regression?

You know how sometimes you have one of those days which should probably be wiped off the memory slate? Yesterday was one of them for me. In the morning we walked in the forest and at one point I slipped under the fence, spotted an open garden gate and trotted in to say hello. By the time Boss had climbed over the fence and stormed after me I was just emerging from the kitchen with a very friendly man ("I thought I'd acquired another dog!" he laughed) and a collie. The collie kept snapping at me which I thought was hilarious so I bounced and pounced and pranced around her until Boss grabbed me and, with profuse apologies, hauled me away. I spent the rest of the walk in the lead which was even more miserable than it might have been because Boss insisted on practising Julie's tedious snail walk. Then in the afternoon Boss left us alone for *hours* and what's a bored young chap supposed to do – except look for trouble? I got the glue stick off the dining room table ("If you're sick, it serves you right!") and a notepad, retrieved Boss's shoes from the hall and a brush from the fireplace, read the newspaper from cover to cover and pulled the cushions off the armchair. I didn't actually chew any of them, except for a bit of her address book. Of course by the time she deigned to return I'd completely forgotten how I'd amused myself and when she crossly picked up the remains of the address book I had absolutely no idea why she seemed to think it was anything to do with me. "Beau, you never used to do this when you were left alone. You are regressing," she sighed in despair. I have no idea what that means but something tells me it's not complimentary...

Admirers galore

I've got quite good at doing the snail walk round the Common and along the lanes so today Boss took me to town where there are more distractions. This proved a lot harder for both of us as nearly everybody stopped and said wasn't I gorgeous/handsome/lovely etc etc. And even those who didn't stop and speak simply smiled and wafted a hand over my head in passing. How did they know I wouldn't bite?

Flatcoats *are* different

Boss and I have certainly worked on our homework and I know she was hoping it would be apparent in last night's gun dog class. (The trouble with such a small class is that there is no hiding place). We all walked to heel around a small patch of grass while Julie watched us. I must have done all right because she said afterwards she hadn't spoken to us because we seemed to be doing fine. I was glad I hadn't let Boss down because I do like pleasing her although I appreciate this isn't always apparent. It's just that when I'm on the scent of something (pheasant, rabbit, deer, dog, human, anything) I take off, with no thought of the consequences of getting lost or run over or worse. It's not that I *mean* to be naughty, just that a sort of fog envelopes my brain blotting out all hearing, training, everything. After the heel work Julie went round each dog in turn and threw dummies and balls in front of us which the bosses had to retrieve while we stayed put. This is called learning steadiness. (Are the words steady and Beau mutually exclusive? questions Boss). Then we did some more heelwork but this time learning to sit automatically when our boss stopped or blew the whistle. The whole idea is that eventually we sit on the whistle (metaphorically, you understand), whether at heel or further away. If you remember, I used to be quite good at this so it ought to be a case of revision rather than learning something new. Julie made Boss laugh when she saw me debating whether it was worth sitting or not. "He *is* a flatcoat after all; they're different! A Labrador would plonk itself down by your side but a flatcoat has to think about it!" I don't think I've converted Julie to flatcoats but I always make her laugh; she calls me "a very special numpty!" Finally we did some "stays" which as you know used to be my forte but these were very long – longer than I've ever done – so I did fidget a bit but then so did the others. A new man and his Labrador joined the class so now we are six and would you believe, I am the only boy in a class of girls!

Bowing out

A year ago today I arrived at my new home with Boss and Rosco. What an action-packed year it has been! Could any other puppy have done so much in just 12 months! I have swum (or tried to swim) in lakes, rivers, the sea and even a pool; climbed mountains; walked on beaches, the heath and in the forest. I have been to shoots and discovered the thrill of gun dog work. I have been on a train under the Channel, stayed in hotels and travelled through France and around Spain. I have been to school and learned what sit, stay, wait, down and the whistle mean (that is not to say, you understand, that I actually *do* these things all of the time – just that I know what they mean). I have been in loads of pubs and almost as many churches and been blessed by a vicar. I know that I really landed on my paws when I went to live with Boss and Rosco. She is far from perfect but there are worse and I have to admit she is firm but fair and I feel secure knowing that I am deeply loved – whatever problems I may cause her. Of course Rosco is my very best friend but I have made other good friends too like Bella and Rowley and met pigs, sheep, horses, cows and deer. I've even caught a rabbit! On the minus side, I've been at death's door, had two anaesthetics, an X ray and an operation. Hopefully that's all in the past now and I just have loads of good stuff to look forward to. I shall continue with the gun dog classes which finish in July with a fun training day although Boss is keeping an open mind at the moment as to whether we go as she thinks my idea of fun may not coincide with anybody else's. And then in the autumn I shall join Rosco again on the shoot and perhaps be allowed to do the occasional retrieve myself – if I behave. We're soon off to France again and perhaps to Scotland to fish! This blog was only ever intended to chart the exploits of my first year so now I am signing off. But thanks to all of you who have emailed to say reading about my adventures has brought a smile to your face and made your day. Lots of love to you all...XXX

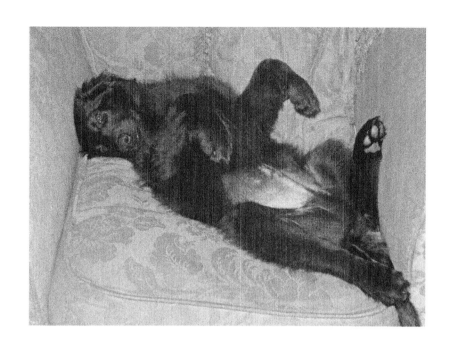

Chillax!

Boss has the last word

"God you need the patience of a saint to train one of these!" laughed Julie, an experienced trainer and owner of working spaniels and Labradors, as she grappled with Beau. Flatcoats have a reputation for being hard to train – largely because they always know best! Perhaps lulling me into a false sense of confidence, Titus and Rosco seemed remarkably easy to train so the challenge of Beau came as a shock. And left me wondering whether I was just lucky with those two and if Beau is in fact normal for the breed...

In the motorway of life, Beau is permanently careering along in the fast lane. He has an exuberant zest for life, grabbing it with all four paws and living every second as though it were his last. The way he's going, this may well prove a sensible policy! I worry for him: that he will be shot, run over, kicked by a horse, dognapped, knock a child or elderly person over, be trampled by a cow, run into the jaws of a hellhound. The possibilities are endless and dire. His boundless self-confidence and inability to listen make him a liability - to say nothing of an exhausting walking companion – and something had to be done. (Of course I could keep him on a lead all the time like so many owners but I feel that not only is this an admission of failure but also unfair for a young active dog).

Beau has not been easy – the question is why? I have investigated him as well as me for answers. Within the first few days, I suspected that he had not been handled very much and research has shown that a lack of socialisation in those crucial early weeks can have devastating behavioural consequences later. The lack of attention was understandable, bearing in mind he was one of 10 puppies with another eight dogs in the household and two owners with full time jobs. The fact that he didn't cry even on the first night here worried me - unlike Rosco who not only screamed for the first three and a half nights but yelled in the car on the way home for a couple of hours before finally collapsing asleep. In contrast, Beau didn't seem too bothered whether I was there or not. He soon attached himself to Rosco but it took a surprisingly long time for him to show any affection to me. I have never previously experienced this with any of my dogs although I can understand why Beau would think Rosco is more fun than me – because he *is* more fun! Unlike me, he doesn't get cross and is always up for a game.

Beau's reluctance to toe the line meant I had to question whether he actually understood what I was asking of him. When owners have complained to me that their dog doesn't listen or is plain stupid or disobedient I have always advised that they stop and look at themselves before blaming the dog. Does the dog understand the command, is the owner giving conflicting messages (like calling the dog back with an aggressive body stance)? Other trainers who observed Beau came to the conclusion that he did indeed understand what was wanted and that defiance rather than misapprehension was the problem.

I also asked myself whether I was the right owner for Beau. Would he be better behaved with someone else? Over the years I have encountered situations where there is nothing wrong with the owner, nothing wrong with the dog but together they are unworkable. Many have commented on the fact that I am quite small and slender and softly spoken. Using physical force and shouting (I only ever "growl" to indicate disapproval) is not my modus operandi but perhaps that was what Beau needed? Some trainers suggested that I sent him away to be trained on the basis that a short sharp shock was what he needed to bring him to his senses. But many gun dog trainers are extremely brutal and not only is it possible to ruin forever a dog with the wrong treatment but I also believe there is never, ever a justification for harsh physical punishment. "Breaking" was the term used for centuries and many still use it. They would do well to heed the words of gun dog expert HH in 1920: "A good shrill whistle, a good stout whip, a check cord and spiked collar for emergencies, and a plentiful command of language, and the thing is done. Is it? Follow this system and succeed in your object, and in nine cases out of ten you get a sulky slave, a senseless automaton, a mechanical apparatus. It may serve its turn, do its business as long as no complication occurs, but the moment you want something out of the common, presence of mind, thought of great courage and perseverance, you are nowhere." The other disadvantage of sending a dog away for training is that then he is trained to work for somebody else – but where does that leave you, the untrained owner?

145

Comparisons are odious and memory can play false tricks: did I expect too much of him, to be another Titus or Rosco? It would be easy to remember Titus as perfect but he was certainly not! If the breed has a problem trait it is their assumption that all and sundry will be love them and in this respect Titus was a typical flatcoat. An article in The Field magazine of 1909 described flatcoats as "*very friendly and affectionate with master and everyone else...*" But at least Titus didn't jump up at strangers. Although I liked the family connection, I was well aware that Titus was a one-off and I neither wanted nor expected a reincarnation. It would be easy too to compare him unfavourably with the largely obedient and very biddable Rosco but, although they are the same breed, they are very different personalities and I have always believed there is more variation within a breed than between breeds.

They say that familiarity breeds contempt and absence makes the heart grow fonder ... I questioned whether Beau spent too much time with me. Would he love and respect me more if he saw less of me? But working from home, I have always spent a lot of time with my dogs. Some trainers suggested that I kennel him on the very logical and sound basis that if you spend 22 hours out of every 24 shut away in a kennel, when you do finally get out you will be ecstatic and ready to do your owner's bidding. I accept the truth in this argument but I have never kennelled my dogs – what is the point of sitting cosily in front of the fire while they are outside? Instead, I opted to go in the opposite direction: to spend *more t*ime with Beau, with more intensive one-to-one training.

Over the years I have not only trained my own dogs (two dachshunds, a Newfoundland, a Labrador, two setter/golden retriever crosses, a Battersea reject, a springer and, of course, two flatcoats) but also helped hundreds of clients with theirs. As a dog psychologist, clients always assume I have perfectly trained dogs. They are immensely reassured when I point out that I don't! True, I've never had a dog with a serious problem like aggression but perfect? Absolutely not.

My training philosophy has always been very simple: to build a close bond based on mutual respect, communication and co-operation, with every training programme tailored to the individual dog's temperament. One size certainly does *not* fit all when it comes to dog training. The desired behaviour is rewarded (preferably with praise rather than food) and inappropriate behaviour "punished" by withdrawal of attention.

I'm Boss in the blog because that is what I am. I am not pack leader because that implies I am a dog and my dogs are quite smart enough to know that I am not one of them. I am their companion but not their friend because that suggests equality and we are not equal. Friends don't tell each other what to do – well, not if they want to maintain the friendship! And I am emphatically not their "mummy" and I cringe whenever I hear an owner refer to herself as such. One trainer I know calls herself a guardian rather than an

147

owner, arguing that dogs are like children – ie we don't own them. In my opinion, she has missed a massive difference in the raising of dogs and children. Our role as parents is to teach our children independence so that that in time they are sufficiently confident to fly the nest and explore the world. That is the very last thing I want my dog to do! In the eyes of the law, whether we have bought the dog or been given it, we are the owner. I regard us as a family firm working as a team. I am the boss in that I give the orders and expect obedience in a companionable relationship based on mutual trust and respect.

The good news is that as Beau passes through the toddler tantrums we are turning the corner. But I have to confess I have resorted to the kind of help that I never dreamed I would use. I invested in a spray collar; the idea of this is that when the dog does something undesirable – in Beau's case, rush off after people and dogs – you give him a quick zap of citronella. It worked like magic! He was so shocked by this strange smell that it stopped him in his tracks. I only needed to use it for a short while, and very sparingly, and he soon remembered to stop on the whistle alone.

To start with, I walked Beau and Rosco separately because each was better behaved without the other to egg him on but now that Beau is finally beginning to listen and pay attention and keep closer, the three of us usually walk together. We walk on and off the lead and he is learning not to throw himself at people; he looks longingly at them desperately trying to catch their eye but with four paws attached to the ground. When he starts to stray too far off the path, the words "this way" and a point in the right direction bring him back. Generally his recall is OK although I would like him to return a little more quickly – rather than his casual lollop back. But I must be patient. The training is immensely time consuming and hard work but for his safety and my sanity we have to continue. Yes, there are occasional relapses when Dr Jekyll slips back into Mr Hyde - but they are getting fewer.

I laugh now when I think how once I worried that he was not attached! Now I could not have a more devoted companion. When I am sitting in the armchair, he leans up against my leg and wallops me with a big black paw. On the sofa he crawls on to my lap oblivious to the fact that he no longer fits. In the garden, he sits on my heels while I am weeding or bakes in the heat when I am sunbathing rather than sensibly retreating into the shade. Wherever I am, there is Beau, my guardian angel.

I have learned a great deal from Beau and he has been good for me in my work. A dog psychologist is always a client's last desperate resort and of course I have felt compassion for them and their "problem" dog but the wilful, wayward Beau has given me a new empathic insight into just what a failure a dog can make an owner feel!

Beau has brought me another unwelcome first. While other puppies in the class were going through a destructive stage, I could leave Beau home alone confident that he wouldn't chew anything.

But just as the others grew out of their destructive behaviour, Beau decided to adopt it. (They do say that flatcoats are late developers!) Out of the blue, he decided he'd like to learn to read, happily helping himself to some of my books, pulling out two or three at a time and devouring the spines and a few pages, lending new meaning to the term dog-eared. This was a new experience for me. (Rosco once chewed a bit of skirting board but after I covered it with chilli powder and mustard the next day, he never touched it again). I wondered whether Beau had developed anxiety at being left home alone (it is thought that as many 80% of Britain's 10 million dogs develop problem behaviour for this reason) so one day I left a camcorder running. It was fascinating. Beau climbed on the armchair (allowed) and sighed heavily, then got off and looked on the dining room table (not allowed) and then the kitchen table (also not allowed) to see if I had been stupid enough to leave anything within reach. No luck so he went and looked out of the window. Not a lot to see there so back on to the armchair and another huge sigh. It was a wonderful impression of a very bored dog looking for trouble rather than one suffering from separation anxiety. I have never crated my dogs but Beau has left me thinking that I may have to – if I am to have any books left.

As regards Beau's deformed back legs I have decided to adopt a wait and see policy. I chose not to re-X ray him when he was a year old because it would have meant yet another anaesthetic. At the moment he does not appear to be in any pain although of course one can never be certain of this; he may be stoically putting up with discomfort because he knows no different. But judging by the way he runs and jumps it seems unlikely that he is suffering a great deal. If that changes we will re-think. But the only way to fix bowed femurs is a fairly gruesome operation whereby the bones are cut and re-aligned; in addition the hip joints would need to be replaced with implants. How does one explain to a young dog why you are subjecting him to so much pain and misery – when there are no guarantees of success? Herein lies a moral and ethical dilemma: just because you can do something does not necessarily mean that you should.

Beau is not insured so the cost is obviously a factor although not an insurmountable one; if I was convinced that operating was the best answer, the money would be found. Over the years, I have been lucky that my dogs have been remarkably healthy and insurance would have been a costly waste of money. Choosing not to insure Beau was obviously not one of my best decisions in the light of his numerous problems – but the way I look at it is that he using up all those premiums I would have paid over the years!

The jury is still out as to whether he will ever make a gun dog. He currently shows little interest in retrieving. At the classes, all the other youngsters joyfully bring back the dummy whereas Beau is super-keen to go and get it but then ... either drops it and wanders off or disappears into the long grass with it! The only exceptions are when water is involved and suddenly he decides that retrieving is the greatest game of all or when I do a passable imitation of an Indian war dance which might astonish onlookers but encourages him to return with the dummy. It would be lovely to think that one day he will take over from Rosco on the shoot as retrieving is what flatcoats were bred for. I take comfort from the words of gun dog judge and author Colonel David Hancock: "Some wayward individuals when young have become quite outstanding performers when mature. The skill of the gifted trainer is in acknowledging individuality." But if his trainer is not sufficiently gifted or his legs let him down, Beau will always have a loving home with me.

Would I have bought him if I had met his breeder first or known of his various medical problems? No. (And I will always wonder whether the would-be owner before me really did reject him just because he had been chipped – or did she spot something else?). But I have no regrets. Despite being such hard work and an excruciating embarrassment at times, Beau has brought a huge amount of fun and laughter into my life and I wouldn't be without him for the world.

Best buddies: Rosco and Beau

The Cruel and Unexpected End

When I finished this book, it never occurred to me that Beau and I would not have a brilliant future, building on the unshakeable bond we had formed. So when he was diagnosed with a particularly aggressive multi focal cancer at only 17 months it was a shocking, devastating blow. Five days after the diagnosis, I cradled Beau in my arms as he slipped, unaware, into the darkness.

Sometimes Rosco and I sit on the beach watching the jet black cormorants skimming the waves and imagine that they are the free spirits of the boys we loved and lost.

Titus enjoyed 13 full, happy years but Beau was denied the chance to grow up, let alone grow old – although his pitifully short time was certainly packed with action. As news of his tragically early death spread, it became clear that, through his blog, he had endeared himself to an astonishing number of people, many of them strangers. Emails, cards, letters and even flowers flooded in. Despite his frequent and sometimes painful visits to vet Jenny, he was always thrilled to see her and I was deeply touched by the card she sent after putting him to sleep in the garden: "I will never forget what a wonderful like-able dog Beau was and he has you to thank for bringing that out in him."

Now my beautiful Beau sleeps peacefully beside his predecessor Titus beneath the old rose, Beau Narcise. He has gone but he lives on. Wherever I walk, there is a trio of flat-coats beside me, one of which will be forever a puppy.

Printed in Great Britain
by Amazon

59237808R00092